Volume equivalents

METRIC	IMPERIAL	METRIC	IMPERIAL
30ml	1fl oz	450ml	15fl oz
60ml	2fl oz	500ml	16fl oz
75ml	2$\frac{1}{2}$fl oz	600ml	1 pint
100ml	3$\frac{1}{2}$fl oz	750ml	1$\frac{1}{4}$ pints
120ml	4fl oz	900ml	1$\frac{1}{2}$ pints
150ml	5fl oz ($\frac{1}{4}$ pint)	1 litre	1$\frac{3}{4}$ pints
175ml	6fl oz	1.2 litres	2 pints
200ml	7fl oz ($\frac{1}{3}$ pint)	1.4 litres	2$\frac{1}{2}$ pints
240ml	8fl oz	1.5 litres	2$\frac{3}{4}$ pints
300ml	10fl oz ($\frac{1}{2}$ pint)	1.7 litres	3 pints
350ml	12fl oz	2 litres	3$\frac{1}{2}$ pints
400ml	14fl oz	3 litres	5$\frac{1}{4}$ pints

Weight equivalents

METRIC	IMPERIAL	METRIC	IMPERIAL
15g	$\frac{1}{2}$oz	150g	5$\frac{1}{2}$oz
20g	$\frac{3}{4}$oz	175g	6oz
25g	scant 1oz	200g	7oz
30g	1oz	225g	8oz
45g	1$\frac{1}{2}$oz	250g	9oz
50g	1$\frac{3}{4}$oz	300g	10oz
60g	2oz	450g	1lb
75g	2$\frac{1}{2}$oz	500g	1lb 2oz
85g	3oz	675g	1$\frac{1}{2}$lb
100g	3$\frac{1}{2}$oz	900g	2lb
115g	4oz	1kg	2$\frac{1}{4}$lb
125g	4$\frac{1}{2}$oz	1.5kg	3lb 3oz
140g	5oz	1.8kg	4lb

everyday
easy
30-minute
Suppers

everyday easy
30-minute Suppers

off the shelf • quick assembly • fresh and light

DK

LONDON, NEW YORK, MELBOURNE,
MUNICH, AND DELHI

Designer
Elma Aquino

Editorial Assistant
Shashwati Tia Sarkar

Senior Jacket Creative
Nicola Powling

Managing Editors
Dawn Henderson, Angela Wilkes

Managing Art Editor
Christine Keilty

Production Editor
Maria Elia

Production Controller
Hema Gohil

Creative Technical Support
Sonia Charbonnier

DK INDIA

Head of Publishing
Aparna Sharma

Editors
Dipali Singh, Saloni Talwar

Designer
Devika Dwarkadas

DTP Co-ordinator
Sunil Sharma

DTP Designer
Tarun Sharma

Material first published in *The Cooking Book*, 2008
and *Cook Express*, 2009
This edition first published in Great Britain in 2010
by Dorling Kindersley Limited
80 Strand, London WC2R 0RL

A Penguin Company
Copyright © 2008, 2009, 2010 Dorling Kindersley
Text copyright © 2008, 2009, 2010 Dorling Kindersley

2 4 6 8 10 9 7 5 3 1
005 - CD263 - May/10

A CIP catalogue record for this book
is available from the British Library.

ISBN 978-1-4053-5524-7

Colour reproduction by MDP, Bath
Printed and bound in China by Leo

Discover more at
www.dk.com

CONTENTS

INTRODUCTION

Fast food that is good food – surely that is the holy grail for all of us? Sometimes it feels like the last thing we have time for is to cook a meal from scratch and it's all too easy to reach for the additive-laden, ready-prepared meal in the freezer, but preparing delicious, nutritious food doesn't have to be time-consuming. The truth is that oven heating those frozen burgers takes nearly as long as making your own. (Don't believe it? Turn to page 178.)

Many favourite recipes from around the world are often easier, and quicker, to make than they appear. Thailand's famous Pad Thai, Paneer and Peas from India, and the Caribbean classic Rice and Beans can all be made in minutes.

Speedy cooking is made much simpler if you are prepared for those days when you have no time to shop. Having the basics in the house means you can cook up a feast at the shortest notice. The Useful Information section at the start of the book gives invaluable advice on **Stocking Up**: what to fill your storecupboards, fridge, and freezer with, how to store it, and how to use it.

Next, a selection of step-by-step **Techniques** will refine your core cookery skills and help you save on preparation time, whether you are cooking the perfect pasta or preparing a prickly pineapple. These show you the best quick cooking methods, such as grilling, frying, and steaming – all great choices when you need good food, fast – and ingredients, such as eggs, which are one of the best ingredients a time-poor cook can have in stock.

Following this is a range of **Recipe Choosers** that showcase recipes by themes such as Healthy, One-pot, and Vegetarian so cooks in a hurry can easily find something suitable. For those of you who are particularly short of time, look no further than Within 15 minutes!

Simple dishes using minimal ingredients are the centrepieces in the **Fresh and Light** section. There are great ideas for quick assembly meals, such as the classics Waldorf Salad and Caesar Salad, light dishes that are perfect

6

for summer, such as Vegetable Kebabs and Pea and Mint Soup, and feel-good snacks, such as Stuffed Mushrooms and Scrambled Eggs with Smoked Salmon.

When little fresh food seems to be at hand, turn to your storecupboard, fridge, freezer, and the **Off the Shelf** section for inspiration. A jar of olives, a can of beans, a hunk of cheese, some frozen peas – all can be turned into satisfying meals at lightning pace. Using ingredients you can literally take "off the shelf" and just one or two basic fresh ingredients, such as herbs, you can create tasty dishes such as Pasta with Pecorino and Peas or Bean Burgers.

If you're in the mood for something warming and substantial, choose something from the **Hearty and Filling** section. Chicken Fajitas with Tomato and Avocado Salsa and Lamb Koftas are great weeknight fare that you can eat with your fingers, while Cauliflower Cheese and Sweet and Sour Stir-fried Fish with Ginger are guaranteed to be hits with the family.

At the end of a meal, there's no need to spend a lot of effort on the dessert when there are ingenious ideas in the **Quick Puddings** section that deliver instant gratification. Try the Banoffee Pie or Citrus Fruit Salad for sweet treats that need no cooking, while Knickerbocker Glory and Eton Mess are timeless favourites that are sure to be eaten with relish by young and old alike.

The secret of the quickest recipes is to keep things simple. A handful of good ingredients and a stock of good recipes are all you need. It's so easy anyone can do it – day in, day out.

Stocking up

All you need is a well-stocked larder and refrigerator to form the basis of a good meal. When you don't have time to shop, it means there will always be something around to make a quick supper with.

SPICES, HERBS

Paprika is best for pork and chicken dishes. Store for 6 months.
Ground coriander and seeds are best for Indian-style curries. Store for 6 months.
Ground chilli and chilli flakes are best for adding spice and heat to Indian, Thai, and Mediterranean dishes. Store for 6 months.
Ground cumin and seeds can be added to a soup, stew or marinade. Store for 6 months.
Ground cinnamon and sticks are best for chicken and lamb stews. Store for 6 months.
Curry powder is best for chicken, lamb, and beef. Store for 6 months.
Dried herbs such as oregano, thyme, mixed dried herbs, and bay leaves are best for chicken, lamb, and fish dishes, stews, and casseroles. Store for 6 months.

PASTA, RICE, NOODLES

Pasta, in its many shapes and sizes, makes a quick and easy supper, and is best for sauces and bakes. Store for 1 year.
Rice is available in many varieties – basmati, brown, long grain, risotto (arborio or carnaroli), and paella. It is best used in pilaf, kedgeree, salads, and serving as an accompaniment to meat and fish. Store for 6 months.
Noodles are available in a selection of types and thicknesses. You can choose from egg, rice, wheat, and buckwheat noodles. You can even buy straight-to-wok noodles, which require no cooking, just heating through. Best for Asian-style dishes, soups, salads, or stir-fries. Store for 6 months.

PULSES, GRAINS, NUTS, FRUITS

Pulses include canned and dried Puy lentils, red lentils, green lentils, and yellow split peas. Canned and dried chickpeas, kidney beans, and butter beans are always useful. Best for stews, salads, bakes, casseroles, dips, and soups. Store for 1 year.
Grains such as farro, pearl barley, couscous, bulgur wheat, and polenta are best for salads and hotpots. Store for 1 year.
Nuts and seeds include a selection of whole peanuts, walnuts, and cashew nuts, chopped and ground almonds; sesame seeds, sunflower seeds, and pumpkin seeds. They are best for toppings, in salads, and stir-fries. Store for 6 months.
Dried fruit, such as sultanas and raisins, dates, figs, and apricots, can be used in salads and stews. Store for 6 months.

OILS, CONDIMENTS, SAUCES

Oils include olive, sunflower, groundnut, and sesame oil, and are best for dressings, salads, marinades, stir-fries, shallow frying, and baking. Store for 6 months.
Vinegars such as red wine, white wine, rice wine, balsamic, and sherry vinegar are best for salads, dressings, and marinades. Store for 1 year.
Mustards such as English, Dijon, and wholegrain add flavour to dishes and dressings. Store for 1 year.
Pesto and pastes include harissa, tomato paste, and Thai curry paste and are best for curries, stirring into casseroles, or for adding to pasta. Store for 6 months.
Sauces such as soy sauce, fish sauce, Worcestershire sauce, and oyster sauce are best for stir-fries, stews, and casseroles. Store for 1 year.

JARS, CANS, POWDERS

Black and green olives, and small salted **capers** are best for pasta, salads, and dips. Store for 1 year.
Tinned whole or chopped tomatoes and sun-dried tomatoes can be added to stews, casseroles, and pasta sauces. Store for 1 year.

Sweetcorn is best for soups or stews. Store for 1 year.
Tuna and salmon can be stored canned, and are best for pasta, salads, fish cakes, and bakes. Store for 1 year.
Anchovies can be stored or canned in olive oil or salt. They are best for pasta,

salads, casseroles, and stews. Store for 1 year.
Coconut milk is best for Thai curries. Store for 1 year.
Powdered stock (bouillon) is available in chicken, beef, and vegetable form and is best for gravies, sauces, soups, and stews. Store for 1 year.

DAIRY FOODS, EGGS

Milk is best for sauces, batters, and puddings. Whole milk gives the best flavour, but semi-skimmed is the most popular as it contains half the fat of whole. Skimmed is best reserved for drinks. Store for 7 days (or until its use-by date), or freeze for 1 month.

Butter and cheese enrich all hot dishes and cheese adds instant protein to a quick dish. Available in different varieties, they are best for sauces, bakes, baking, and sandwiches. Store for 1 month (or until their use-by date), or freeze for up to 3 months.

Eggs are best kept in the refrigerator, unless you plan to use them within a couple of days of purchase. Use them for omelettes, salads, and sandwiches. Store for 3 weeks (or until their use-by date).

FREEZER FOODS

Vegetables can be bought frozen, but peas and broad beans are the only vegetables that withstand the process without it impairing their flavour. They make a great standby and are best for instant soups. You can even add them to fish or

meat pies, casseroles, or as a meal accompaniment. Store for 6 months.
Meat freezes well in the form of minced beef, lamb, or pork sausages; use it for chilli, ragù, hot dogs and sandwiches. Store for 6 months. Freeze raw meat and

poultry for up to 3 months.
Fish and seafood suitable for freezing include fish fillets (such as haddock, pollack, and salmon) and prawns (shell on or off). They are best for fish pies, stir-fries, and barbecues. Store for 3 months.

A guide to symbols

The recipes in this book are accompanied by symbols that alert you to important information.

 Tells you how many people the recipe serves, or how much is produced.

 Indicates how much time you will need to prepare and cook a dish. Next to this symbol you will also find out if additional time is required for marinating, standing, or cooling. Read the recipe to find out exactly how much extra time to allow.

 Points out a healthy dish – low in fat or has a low GI (Glycemic Index).

 This is especially important, as it alerts you to what has to be done before you can begin to cook the recipe, or to parts of the recipe that may take a long time to complete.

 This denotes that special equipment is required, such as a deep-fat fryer or skewers. Where possible, alternatives are given.

 This symbol accompanies freezing information.

9

TECHNIQUES

Grill

Fish, vegetables, and tender, prime cuts of meat (demonstrated here) are suitable for cooking under the grill, on a barbecue, or on a ridged cast-iron grill pan.

1 Heat the grill pan over a high heat until very hot. Prepare the meat by brushing both sides with oil using a pastry brush. Then, season with a little salt and pepper.

2 Cook the meat for 1 minute, then rotate it 45 degrees to achieve crossing grill marks and cook for another 1–2 minutes. Repeat on the other side. Remove and allow to rest before serving.

Pan-fry

This quick cooking method is best suited to lean cuts of meat, fish (demonstrated here), or tender vegetables. Use a shallow frying pan, and a little oil or fat.

1 Season the fish with salt and pepper. Heat ¹/₂ tbsp olive oil or sunflower oil in a non-stick frying pan until hot (but not spitting). Add the fish, and leave to cook for 2–3 minutes.

2 Turn the fish over, and cook the other side for 2–3 minutes, or longer if the fish fillet is thick. Keep the heat at medium-high. Turn the fish over again (it should be an even golden colour), and serve.

Stir-fry

Stir-frying can be used to cook meat, fish, and vegetables (demonstrated here). Chop your ingredients to the same size, keep the heat high, and stir constantly.

1 Heat the wok or large frying pan over a medium-high heat, then add $^1/_2$ tbsp vegetable or sunflower oil. Heat until hot and sizzling. Add any spices first, and stir-fry vigorously for a minute.

2 Add the vegetables in order of firmness (firmest first). Continue stirring so the vegetables don't burn. Stir-fry for 4–5 minutes until the vegetables are cooked. Season well, and serve.

Steam

Steaming is a healthy way to cook vegetables, meat, and fish (demonstrated here), and ensures none of the flavours are lost during cooking.

1 To use a bamboo steamer, pour water into a wok to just below where the steamer fits. Add any flavourings, then bring to a simmer. Put the basket in the wok, but ensure the base is above the water.

2 Steam the fish with any extra flavourings until opaque and flaking easily. Allow 3–4 minutes for fillets, 6–8 minutes for fish up to 340g (12oz), and 12–15 minutes for fish up to 900g (2lb).

Soak and cook rice

To cook perfect rice, use $1^{1}/_{2}$ times as much water or stock as rice.
Always be sure to soak and rinse the rice before cooking.

Put rice and liquid into a large saucepan.
Over a medium heat, bring to the boil, stir once, and lower the heat to simmer uncovered for 10–12 minutes, or until all the liquid is absorbed. Remove from the heat and cover with a clean, folded towel, and a fitted lid on top of that. Leave the rice to steam, without removing the lid, for 20 minutes. Remove the folded towel and replace the lid. Leave the rice to sit for 5 minutes, covered. Fluff the rice with a fork and serve.

Boil noodles

While rice noodles only need to be soaked in hot water before use, other noodles need to be boiled. Rinsing under cold water refreshes them.

1 To boil egg, wheat, or buckwheat noodles, bring a large saucepan of water to the boil. Add the noodles, return to the boil, then cook until the noodles are softened and flexible – about 2 minutes.

2 Drain the noodles in a colander and place them under cold, running water. Toss the noodles with a little oil to prevent them from sticking, then serve or proceed with the desired recipe.

Cook dried pasta

Dried pasta is essential to have in your storecupboard as it can form the basis of many quick dishes, but it's all too easy to overcook it.

1 Bring a large pan of salted water to the boil and gently pour in the pasta. Boil uncovered, following the recommended cook time on the packet, or until *al dente* (cooked, but firm to the bite) when tasted.

2 As soon as the pasta is *al dente*, quickly drain it through a colander, shaking it gently to remove any excess water. Toss the pasta with a little oil, then serve or proceed with the recipe.

Make couscous

With no cooking on the hob or in the oven, couscous is quick and easy to prepare. Use around 1³/₄ times as much water as couscous.

1 Pour the quick-cook couscous and a pinch of salt into a large bowl and pour over boiling water. Cover with a folded tea towel, leave for 5 minutes, remove the tea towel, and fluff up with a fork.

2 Re-cover the bowl and leave for another 5 minutes. Remove the tea towel and add either 1 tbsp olive oil or a knob of unsalted butter and fluff up the couscous again until light. Serve.

Test eggs for freshness

As well as the best-before date on the egg box, you can use this simple test to check how fresh your eggs are: immerse the egg in water and see if it rises. A stale egg contains much more air and less liquid than a fresh one, so it will float. Do not use a stale egg.

Fresh

Borderline

Stale

Boil eggs

Despite the name, eggs must be simmered – never boiled. If a green ring appears, it is the result of overcooking (or an old egg).

For soft-boiled

The whites are set and the yolks runny. In a deep pan, cover the eggs with cold water and bring to boil. Lower to a simmer for 2–3 minutes.

For hard-boiled

Both the whites and yolks are set. Simmer for 10 minutes from the boil. Place the pan under cold running water to stop cooking; peel when cool.

Scramble eggs

Scramble as you like, whether you prefer your curds large or small. Before you begin, beat the eggs in a bowl, and season with salt and pepper.

1 Heat a non-stick pan over medium heat, then melt a knob of butter to lightly coat the base. When the butter has melted but not yet browned, pour in the beaten eggs.

2 Using a wooden spoon, pull the setting egg from the edges of the pan into the centre to cook the raw egg. For larger curds, let the egg set longer before scrambling.

Make an omelette

A 3-egg omelette is easiest to handle; any more than 6 eggs is difficult. Before you begin, beat the eggs in a bowl, and season with salt and pepper.

1 Heat a non-stick frying pan over a medium heat and melt a knob of butter. Add the eggs, tilting the pan so the eggs can spread evenly. Stir the eggs with a fork to distribute the eggs evenly.

2 Stop stirring the eggs as soon as they are set. Fold the side of the omelette nearest to you halfway over itself. Flip it halfway over again, then slide it on to a plate, and serve immediately.

Segment citrus fruit

Preparing citrus fruit this way ensures clean and precise wedges for a more attractive garnish.

1 Cut the ends off the fruit so it stands upright. Holding it firmly, slice along the contour of the skin, removing as much of the pith as possible.

2 Slice along the lines of the membrane, which separates each slice. Repeat slicing between each membrane until the fruit is fully segmented.

Prepare mango

Cutting into halves along the fibrous stone and "hedgehogging" the mango is the cleanest way to remove the flesh.

1 Stand the mango on its side and cut it just to one side of the stone; repeat on the other side to make 2 halves. A slice containing the stone will remain.

2 Cut the flesh into square segments, cutting to, but not through, the skin. Invert the skin to expose the flesh. Cut along the skin to remove the flesh.

Prepare pineapple

Take care when handling the sharp outer skin, and use the sharpest knife you can find as the inner core is tough.

1 Top and tail the pineapple. Stand it on its base, and slice the skin from the top down, all the way around the fruit.

2 Cut it in half lengthways, then into wedges, and slice away the fibrous core that runs through the centre of the fruit.

Prepare pomegranate

This delicious Middle Eastern fruit has a tough skin and requires patience when preparing, but it's worth the effort.

1 Slice the fruit into quarters with a sharp knife. The juicy, red seeds are clustered and divided by thin, pithy membranes that are bitter to taste.

2 Over a bowl, gently invert each quarter to make the seeds come loose. Pick out any seeds that remain. Remove any membranes and discard.

Healthy

Bean burgers page 114

Baked white fish in wine and herbs page 72

Leaf-wrapped Asian sole page 42

Thai-style minced pork page 186

Lentil, broad bean, and feta salad page 88

Sweet and sour stir-fried fish with ginger page 168

Chinese dumplings page 70

Pea and mint soup page 80

Vegetarian Pad Thai page 90

Hot and sour beef stir-fry with green beans page 188

Tuna and white beans with olives page 104

Vietnamese salad of grilled prawns with papaya page 44

One-pot

Seared duck page 180

Rice and beans page 122

Linguine alle vongole page 92

Kidneys with mustard sauce
page 134

Orechiette with pancetta
page 56

Pasta with mushroom sauce
page 172

Pasta with pecorino and peas
page 106

Mussels in fennel broth page 140

Vegetarian Pad Thai page 90

Lamb with blueberries page 136

Kasha pilaf page 84

Spiced orzo with spinach
page 82

Minced chicken with exotic mushooms, soy, and lime page 146

Kässpätzle page 98

Vegetarian

Cauliflower cheese page 174

Vegetable kebabs page 76

Egg noodles with lemon and herbs page 78

Waldorf salad page 52

Kässpätzle page 98

Rice and beans page 122

Gnocchi with Gorgonzola and walnut sauce page 110

Fettucine Alfredo page 94

Paneer and peas page 116

Pasta with olives, capers, and sun-dried tomatoes page 118

Kasha pilaf page 84

Asparagus, broccoli, ginger, and mint stir-fry page 150

Grated courgette and goat's cheese omelette page 66

Stuffed mushrooms page 36

Tomato and harissa tart page 156

Spiced orzo with spinach page 82

Cold

Lentils with artichokes and peppers page 108

Couscous with pine nuts and almonds page 74

Tuna and white beans with olives page 104

Waldorf salad page 52

Crab salad page 48

Layered marinated herring salad page 34

Tomato bulgur wheat with capers and olives page 100

Pea and mint soup page 80

Lobster salad with watercress page 60

Lentil, broadbean, and feta salad page 88

Bulgur wheat with mixed peppers, mint, and goat's cheese page 148

Caesar salad page 46

Budget

Rice balls filled with cheese
page 96

Turkey burgers page 182

Caesar salad page 46

Black pudding with apples page 142

Egg fu yung page 112

Simple cheese omelette page 40

Frikadeller page 130

Egg and fennel potato salad
page 170

Waldorf salad page 52

Welsh rarebit page 120

Pork escalopes page 184

Hamburgers page 178

Within 15 minutes – Savoury

Egg noodles with lemon and herbs page 78

Grilled halibut with green sauce page 54

Crab salad page 48

Couscous with pine nuts and almonds page 74

Caesar salad page 46

Simple cheese omelette page 40

Lentils with artichokes and peppers page 108

Within 15 minutes – Sweet

Banoffee pie page 220

Pear and grape salad page 214

Zabaglione page 192

Knickerbocker glory page 218

Pear gratin page 210

Warm fruit compôte page 198

Eton mess page 194

31

FRESH AND LIGHT

Layered marinated herring salad

For convenience, and to save time, buy ready-marinated herring fillets.

INGREDIENTS

1 sweet onion, thinly sliced
250ml (9fl oz) soured cream
120ml (4fl oz) plain yogurt
1 tbsp fresh lemon juice
1/4 tsp caster sugar
2 tart dessert apples, peeled, cored, and thinly sliced
2 pickled dill cucumbers, sliced or chopped
salt and freshly ground black pepper
300g (10oz) marinated herring fillets, drained
2 cooked potatoes, diced (optional)
1 cooked beetroot, sliced (optional)
1 tbsp chopped dill, to garnish

METHOD

1 Put the onion in a bowl, cover with cold water, and leave to soak for 15 minutes. Drain well, then toss with the soured cream, yogurt, lemon juice, and sugar. Stir in the apple and pickles, and season to taste with salt and pepper.

2 Place half the herring in a serving dish and top with the potatoes and the beetroot, if using. Cover with half the soured cream sauce. Layer the remaining herring, potatoes, and beetroot over the sauce, then add the remaining sauce.

3 Cover the dish tightly with cling film and refrigerate. Sprinkle with dill just before serving.

GOOD WITH Slices of sourdough bread or pumpernickel.

PREPARE AHEAD The salad benefits from being assembled up to 2 days in advance and chilled.

serves 6–10

prep 15 mins,
plus soaking
and chilling

Stuffed mushrooms

Field mushrooms, or those with open cups, make great bases for fillings.

INGREDIENTS

8 open-cup mushrooms
2 tbsp olive oil, plus extra for greasing
4 shallots, finely chopped
2 garlic cloves, crushed
115g (4oz) pine nuts, toasted
4 tbsp basil, roughly torn
4 tbsp flat-leaf parsley, finely chopped
salt and freshly ground black pepper
175g (6oz) firm goat's cheese
8 slices of pancetta

METHOD

1 Preheat the oven to 190°C (375°F/Gas 5). Place the mushrooms on an oiled baking tray.

2 Heat the olive oil in a large frying pan and fry the shallots over a medium heat for 2–3 minutes, or until softened, stirring frequently. Add the garlic, pine nuts, basil, and parsley, and season to taste with salt and pepper.

3 Spoon the mixture into the mushrooms and top with a slice of goat's cheese.

4 Wrap a slice of pancetta around each mushroom, tucking the ends underneath.

5 Bake for 15–20 minutes, or until the mushrooms are tender and the pancetta is crisp. Serve immediately.

GOOD WITH Young salad leaves and a drizzle of balsamic vinegar.

serves 4

prep 10 mins
• cook 15–20 mins

Scrambled eggs with smoked salmon

This feel-good recipe is great at any time of day.

INGREDIENTS

6 large eggs
2 tbsp milk
salt and freshly ground black pepper
45g (1½oz) unsalted butter
225g (8oz) smoked salmon, cut into thin strips,
   or hot smoked salmon, flaked
2 tbsp snipped chives
4 English muffins, split and toasted, to serve

METHOD

1 Beat the eggs with the milk, and season to taste with salt and pepper.

2 Melt the butter in a medium non-stick saucepan and, when foaming, pour in the eggs. Stir with a wooden spoon over medium heat until almost set, then stir in the smoked salmon.

3 Cook until the eggs have just set, sprinkle with chives, season with pepper, and serve at once on toasted muffin halves.

serves 4

prep 10 mins
• cook 10 mins

Simple cheese omelette

A great omelette is cooked only just to the point of being "done"; a sprinkle of cheese is the perfect finishing touch.

INGREDIENTS
2 eggs
drop of milk
salt and freshly ground black pepper
1 tbsp butter
handful of grated cheese

METHOD
1 Crack the eggs into a bowl and lightly whisk with a drop of milk. Season with salt and pepper.

2 Heat a small frying pan over a medium heat until hot, then add the butter. Once the butter is melted and foaming, pour in the egg mixture. Pull the edges away from the side of the pan using a spatula or fork; keep doing this so that any uncooked mixture runs to the edge. After about 30 seconds, most of the egg should be set. It will still be soft in the middle, but residual heat will continue cooking the omelette after it is taken out of the pan.

3 Sprinkle the cheese down the centre of the omelette, then fold one half of the omelette over the top of the other. Slide on to a plate, and serve immediately.

GOOD WITH A fresh, mixed leaf salad.

serves 1

prep 2 mins
• cook 1 min

Leaf-wrapped Asian sole

Steaming fish ensures the flavours are retained. Here, ginger and soy sauce add intensity.

INGREDIENTS

4 sole fillets, about 175g (6oz) each
4 tsp lemon juice
4 tsp soy sauce
2 tsp grated fresh root ginger
sesame oil, for drizzling
16–20 large pak choi leaves, tough stalks removed

METHOD

1 Drizzle each sole fillet with 1 tsp lemon juice, 1 tsp soy sauce, $\frac{1}{2}$ tsp ginger, and a light, even drizzle of sesame oil. Gently roll the fillets lengthways and arrange them on a heatproof plate.

2 Fill a large saucepan fitted with a steamer rack with 2.5cm (1in) water; bring to the boil, then reduce the heat to a simmer.

3 In a separate pan of simmering water, blanch the pak choi leaves for several seconds, or until soft, then drain and refresh briefly in a bowl of iced water. Drain again.

4 Wrap each rolled fillet in 4–5 pak choi leaves, securing with cocktail sticks if necessary. Set the plate with the fish on the steamer rack, place the lid on the steamer, and steam for 8–10 minutes, or until the fish is opaque.

GOOD WITH A mix of stir-fried vegetables, or boiled white rice.

serves 4

prep 15 mins
• cook 10 mins

healthy option

large saucepan
fitted with a
steamer rack
• cocktail sticks

Vietnamese salad of grilled prawns with papaya

Lime, mint, and papaya create the fresh, clean flavours of this salad.

INGREDIENTS

12 large raw prawns
2 tbsp vegetable oil
1 tsp rice wine vinegar
1 tsp sugar
1 red chilli, deseeded and very finely chopped
2 garlic cloves, crushed
2 tbsp Vietnamese fish sauce
   or Thai fish sauce, such as nam pla
1 tbsp lime juice
1 tbsp chopped *rau ram* (Vietnamese mint)
   or mint leaves, plus extra sprigs to garnish
1 green papaya, deseeded, quartered
   lengthways, and thinly sliced
1/2 cucumber, deseeded and cut into thin strips

METHOD

1 Peel and devein the prawns, removing and discarding the heads and tails. Spread them out on a foil-lined grill rack, brush with the oil, and grill for 2–3 minutes, or until they turn pink.

2 Meanwhile, whisk the rice wine vinegar, sugar, chilli, garlic, fish sauce, lime juice, and 75ml (2½fl oz) cold water together in a bowl until the sugar dissolves. Add the cooked prawns to the bowl and stir well until they are coated in the dressing. Leave to cool completely.

3 Add the chopped mint, papaya, and cucumber and toss together. Transfer the salad to a serving platter, with the prawns on the top, and garnish with mint sprigs.

PREPARE AHEAD Steps 1 and 2 can be completed up to several hours in advance. Store, covered, in the refrigerator, until ready to serve.

serves 4

prep 15 mins
• cook 2–3 mins

healthy option

44

Caesar salad

Anchovies and Parmesan cheese give this salad its distinctive, salty flavour.

INGREDIENTS

2 small heads of Cos lettuce, torn into small pieces
100g (3$^{1}/_{2}$oz) shop-bought croutons
2 large eggs
60g (2oz) Parmesan cheese, shaved or grated

For the dressing

2 garlic cloves, crushed to a purée
2 anchovy fillets in olive oil, drained and finely chopped
120ml (4fl oz) extra virgin olive oil
1 tbsp fresh lemon juice
1 tsp Worcestershire sauce
freshly ground black pepper

METHOD

1 To make the dressing, mash the garlic and anchovies together to make a thick paste. Transfer to a screw-top jar, add the olive oil, lemon juice, and Worcestershire sauce, then season to taste with pepper. Shake the dressing until well blended. Set aside.

2 To assemble the salad, toss the lettuce leaves with the croutons in a salad bowl. Bring a small saucepan of water to the boil over a high heat. Reduce the heat to medium, add the eggs, and boil gently for no more than 2 minutes. Drain and rinse with cold water.

3 Crack open the eggs, scoop on to the lettuce, and toss. Shake the dressing again, then add to the salad, and toss again. Sprinkle with the Parmesan and serve at once.

GOOD WITH All barbecued meats. It is especially good served with chunks of French bread.

PREPARE AHEAD The dressing can be made in advance; keep chilled in an airtight container for up to 1 week.

serves 6

prep 10 mins
• cook 2 mins

Crab salad

Crab works really well with fruity flavours; this is a lovely summer dish.

INGREDIENTS
few mint leaves, roughly chopped
handful of coriander leaves, roughly chopped
handful of mixed salad leaves, such as rocket,
    spinach, and watercress
1 shallot, finely chopped
350g (12oz) fresh crab, white and
    brown meat separated
1 ripe avocado, sliced lengthways

For the dressing
1 ripe mango, roughly chopped
zest and juice of $1/2$ lime
3 tbsp olive oil

METHOD
1 To make the dressing, put the mango, lime zest and juice, and olive oil in a food processor and process until smooth. Add a little water if too thick.

2 To make the salad, mix together the herbs with the salad leaves. Add the shallot and toss the salad leaves in a little of the dressing. Divide the salad between 4 plates and arrange a spoonful each of the white and brown crabmeat. Serve with the avocado slices and the remaining dressing on the side.

GOOD WITH Slices of warm soda bread, or brown bread and butter.

serves 4

prep 15 mins

purchase the
crab on the day
you intend to
make the salad

food processor

Chicken poached in coconut milk

Give chicken a fragrant flavour by cooking it in this rich broth.

INGREDIENTS

8 chicken breast fillets, skin on,
    about 200g (7oz) each
500ml (16fl oz) hot light
    vegetable stock
400ml can coconut milk
3 bay leaves
3 garlic cloves, peeled
salt and freshly ground black pepper

METHOD

1 To poach the chicken, put the chicken breasts in a large lidded pan over a medium heat, then pour over the hot stock and the coconut milk. Add the bay leaves, garlic cloves, and season with salt and pepper. Bring to the boil, then cover the pan, reduce the heat slightly, and simmer for 10–15 minutes until the chicken is cooked. Poke a sharp knife into the thickest part of the flesh to check – the juices should run clear.

2 Using a slotted spoon, remove the chicken from the pan, and leave to cool for a minute or two. When cool enough to handle, discard the skin, either slice the chicken or shred using two forks, and serve with a little of the coconut poaching liquid.

GOOD WITH Any rice, but especially boiled basmati rice.

serves 4

prep 5 mins
• cook 15 mins

Waldorf salad

A classic dish named after the prestigious Waldorf-Astoria hotel in New York.

INGREDIENTS

500g (1lb 2oz) crisp, red-skinned apples, cored and diced
juice of ½ lemon
4 celery sticks, thickly sliced crossways
150ml (5fl oz) mayonnaise
salt and freshly ground black pepper
85g (3oz) walnuts, coarsely chopped
snipped chives, to garnish

METHOD

1 Place the diced apples into a mixing bowl and pour the lemon juice on top. Coat the apple well, as this will prevent discolouring.

2 Add the celery, mayonnaise, and season to taste with salt and pepper. Mix well, then cover and chill.

3 Remove the salad from the refrigerator, stir in the walnuts, sprinkle with the chives, and serve.

serves 4

prep 20 mins,
plus chilling

Grilled halibut with green sauce

A fresh-tasting dish that is easy to prepare and cooks in minutes.

INGREDIENTS
6 chunky halibut fillets, about 140g (5oz) each
1 tbsp olive oil
salt and freshly ground black pepper
lemon wedges, to serve

For the green sauce
45g (1½oz) mixed herbs, such as parsley,
    chives, mint, tarragon, and chervil
2 garlic cloves
8 tbsp olive oil
1 tbsp tarragon vinegar
salt and freshly ground black pepper
pinch of caster sugar

METHOD
1 Place all the ingredients for the sauce in a food processor, process until smooth, and season to taste with salt and pepper, and the pinch of caster sugar. Chill until needed.

2 Preheat the grill on its highest setting. Lightly brush the halibut with oil, and season to taste with salt and pepper. Cook the fish for 2 minutes on each side, and serve with the green sauce and lemon wedges to squeeze over.

GOOD WITH Boiled potatoes and green beans.

serves 6

prep 10 mins
• cook 4 mins

food processor

Orecchiette with pancetta

Short pastas, such as orecchiette (literally "little ears" in Italian), work well with oil-based dressings.

INGREDIENTS

450g (1lb) dried orecchiette pasta
2 tbsp light olive oil, plus extra for drizzling
175g (6oz) pancetta, chopped
2 courgettes, chopped
3 garlic cloves, crushed
1/2–1 tsp chilli flakes
175g (6oz) frozen peas
salt and freshly ground black pepper
6 tbsp grated pecorino cheese or Parmesan cheese
3 tbsp chopped flat-leaf parsley

METHOD

1 Cook the orecchiette in plenty of lightly salted boiling water for 7–8 minutes, or until cooked but still firm to the bite.

2 Meanwhile, heat the oil in a large frying pan, add the pancetta, and fry until lightly golden. Add the courgettes, garlic, chilli flakes, and frozen peas, and fry for 2–3 minutes, or until the peas are heated through.

3 Drain the cooked orecchiette and add to the frying pan. Season to taste with salt and pepper, and stir well. Scatter over the cheese and parsley. Drizzle with olive oil to serve.

serves 4

prep 10 mins
• cook 10 mins

Salad Niçoise

This famous French classic is suitable for a main course.

INGREDIENTS

150g (5½oz) green beans, trimmed
4 tuna steaks, about 150g (5½oz) each
extra virgin olive oil, for brushing
salt and freshly ground black pepper
8 anchovy fillets in olive oil, drained
1 red onion, finely sliced
250g (9oz) plum tomatoes, quartered lengthways
12 black olives
2 romaine lettuce hearts, trimmed and
   torn into bite-sized pieces
8–10 basil leaves
4 eggs, hard-boiled

For the vinaigrette

2 tsp Dijon mustard
1 garlic clove, finely chopped
3 tbsp white wine vinegar
150ml (5fl oz) extra virgin olive oil
juice of ½ lemon
salt and freshly ground black pepper

METHOD

1 Cook the green beans in a saucepan of gently boiling water, for 3–4 minutes, or until just tender. Drain the beans and quickly place them into a bowl of ice water.

2 Preheat a ridged grill pan over a medium-high heat. Brush the tuna steaks with 1–2 tbsp olive oil and season to taste with salt and pepper. Sear the tuna steaks for 2 minutes on each side. The centres will still be slightly pink. Set the tuna aside. Drain the green beans.

3 Meanwhile, to make the vinaigrette, whisk together the Dijon mustard, garlic, vinegar, olive oil, and lemon juice. Season to taste with salt and pepper.

4 Place the green beans, anchovies, onion, tomatoes, olives, lettuce, and basil in a large bowl. Drizzle with the vinaigrette and gently toss.

5 Divide the salad between 4 plates. Peel and quarter each egg and add them to the plates. Cut each tuna steak in half and arrange both halves on top of the salad.

serves 4

**prep 25 mins
• cook 8 mins**

ridged grill pan

Lobster salad with watercress

A very special summer salad, with an interesting mixture of flavours.

INGREDIENTS

1/2 red onion, finely sliced
1 tsp red wine vinegar
4 cooked lobster tails, halved
1 large bunch of watercress, tough stalks removed
1/2 fennel bulb, very finely sliced
8 sun-dried tomatoes, chopped
fresh herbs, such as chervil, dill,
   or chives, to garnish

For the dressing

1 egg
1 egg yolk
2 tsp Dijon mustard
zest and juice of 1 lemon
400ml (14fl oz) sunflower oil
10g (1/4oz) chervil or chives
salt and freshly ground black pepper

METHOD

1 To make the dressing, place the egg, egg yolk, mustard, and lemon zest and juice into a blender. Blend on a low speed and slowly add the oil. Add the chervil. Season to taste with salt and pepper. Set aside.

2 Place the red onion in a bowl with the vinegar, and leave to stand for 10 minutes.

3 Remove all the meat from the lobster tails, keeping the pieces of meat as whole as possible, then slice them thickly.

4 Arrange the watercress on plates, scatter over the fennel, the drained onion slices, and the tomatoes. Place the lobster meat on top, drizzle over the dressing, and garnish with fresh herbs.

serves 4

prep 20 mins

blender

Mixed fried fish

This works best with firm white fish, but you can also use squid, sliced into rings.

INGREDIENTS
4 tbsp plain flour
salt and freshly ground black pepper
2 eggs, lightly beaten
85g (3oz) dried white breadcrumbs,
   or Panko breadcrumbs (Japanese breadcrumbs)
115g (4oz) cod fillet, skinned
115g (4oz) salmon fillet, skinned
115g (4oz) snapper fillets, skinned
12 raw king prawns, peeled and deveined,
   and heads removed
oil, for deep frying

For the sauce
60g (2oz) rocket, plus extra to serve
1 garlic clove, crushed
100ml (3^1/$_2$fl oz) mayonnaise
1 tsp lemon juice
salt and freshly ground black pepper

METHOD
1 Place all the ingredients for the sauce in a food processor, season to taste with salt and pepper, and process until smooth. Set aside.

2 Season the flour with salt and pepper. Place the flour, beaten eggs, and breadcrumbs in separate dishes. Cut each fish fillet into 4 pieces. Toss the fish and prawns in the flour, then dip in the egg, and coat in breadcrumbs.

3 Heat the oil to 180°C (350°F) in a large pan or deep-fat fryer. Fry the fish in batches for 2–3 minutes, or until crisp and golden. Drain on kitchen paper.

4 Place a few rocket leaves on each serving plate with the fish on top. Serve immediately, with the sauce served alongside.

serves 4

prep 20 mins
• cook 10 mins

food processor

Linguine with scallops

Succulent scallops with a hint of chilli and lime – perfect for entertaining.

INGREDIENTS

400g (14oz) dried linguine
salt and freshly ground black pepper
juice of 1 lime
5 tbsp olive oil, plus extra for brushing
1 red chilli, finely chopped
2 tbsp chopped coriander
12 king scallops

METHOD

1 Cook the linguine in boiling, salted water for 8 minutes, or until cooked but still firm to the bite. Drain and keep warm.

2 While the pasta is cooking, make the dressing: whisk the lime juice with 5 tbsp olive oil. Stir in the chopped chilli and half the chopped coriander. Season with salt and pepper to taste. Toss the dressing with the drained linguine, set aside, and keep warm.

3 Heat a large griddle pan or large, heavy frying pan over a high heat. Brush the scallops with olive oil, place in the pan and sear for 3 minutes, turning once. Do not overcook or the scallops will be tough.

4 Divide the linguine between 4 serving plates and arrange the scallops on top. Serve immediately, with the remaining coriander sprinkled on top.

GOOD WITH Chunks of crusty bread and a side salad of peppery rocket or watercress leaves dressed with olive oil and scattered with Parmesan shavings.

PREPARE AHEAD The dressing in step 2 can be made 1 hour ahead.

serves 4

prep 10 mins
• cook 8 mins

Grated courgette and goat's cheese omelette

Soft goat's cheese has a herbaceous character that suits green vegetables.

INGREDIENTS

3 eggs, lightly beaten
1 small courgette, grated
salt and freshly ground black pepper
knob of butter
50g (1¾oz) soft goat's cheese, crumbled
small handful of thyme leaves,
    to garnish (optional)

METHOD

1 Mix the beaten egg and grated courgette in a jug. Season with salt and a little pepper.

2 Melt the butter in a small non-stick frying pan over a medium-high heat until foaming, then pour in the egg mixture, swirling it around the pan to cover the base. Gently slide a knife under the edges of the omelette.

3 When the omelette is beginning to cook around the edges, scatter the goat's cheese over the top, so that it is covered evenly. Continue cooking until the centre is almost cooked, but still just a little wet. Remove from the heat, and leave for a couple of minutes to set – the retained heat will continue to cook the omelette.

4 Sprinkle over a little pepper, and garnish with thyme leaves (if using). Carefully slide out of the pan, and serve immediately.

serves 1

prep 10 mins
• cook 15 mins

Lemon and soy skewered chicken with hot dipping sauce

This soy-based marinade doesn't need much time to give the chicken a fresh, tangy flavour.

INGREDIENTS

1 stalk lemongrass, tough outer leaves
   removed, finely chopped
juice of 1 lemon
1 tbsp light soy sauce
1 tsp caster sugar
salt and freshly ground black pepper
4 skinless chicken breast or thigh fillets
150g (5½oz) fine rice noodles

For the dipping sauce

4 garlic cloves, grated or finely chopped
4 red chillies, deseeded and finely chopped
1 tbsp rice wine vinegar
pinch of caster sugar
juice of 1 lemon

METHOD

1 Put the lemongrass, lemon juice, soy sauce, and sugar in a bowl. Season with salt and pepper. Cut each chicken fillet in half lengthways, add to the lemongrass mixture, and leave to marinate while you prepare the noodles and dipping sauce.

2 Prepare the rice noodles according to the packet instructions, drain, and keep warm.

3 To make the dipping sauce, put all the ingredients, except the lemon juice, in a small pan. Add 2 tbsp water, and heat gently until the sugar has dissolved – do not boil. Allow to cool, then stir in the lemon juice.

4 Thread the chicken lengthways on to 8 medium skewers, allowing two for each person. Heat a ridged cast-iron grill pan or frying pan until hot. Grill the chicken for 3–4 minutes on each side until cooked through and lightly charred. Serve with the dipping sauce and the rice noodles.

PREPARE AHEAD The dipping sauce can be made several hours in advance. Chill until needed, then bring back to room temperature and stir before serving.

serves 4

prep 15 mins
• cook 10 mins

healthy option

if using wooden or
bamboo skewers,
soak them for 30
mins before use

8 skewers

68

Chinese dumplings

Wontons are steamed Chinese dumplings and great to have ready in the freezer.

INGREDIENTS

175g (6oz) minced pork
2 spring onions, finely chopped
115g (4oz) shiitake mushrooms, finely chopped
1cm (½in) piece of fresh root ginger, peeled and grated
½ tsp sesame oil
1 tbsp chopped coriander leaves
1 tbsp light soy sauce
freshly ground black pepper
20 wonton wrappers
1 egg, beaten
lettuce or napa cabbage, for steaming

METHOD

1 In a bowl, mix together the pork, spring onions, mushrooms, ginger, sesame oil, coriander, and soy sauce. Season with pepper.

2 Place each wonton wrapper on a clean surface and spoon a little of the pork mixture into the centre of each one. Brush the edges lightly with egg, fold the wrapper in half, and crimp the edges to seal.

3 Fill a pan about one-quarter full of water and bring to the boil. Line the steamer with lettuce and add the wontons. Place the steamer on a rack so it sits above the water, cover, and steam for 10 minutes, or until cooked. Serve at once.

GOOD WITH Soy sauce or your favourite dipping sauce.

PREPARE AHEAD Complete steps 1 and 2 to make the wontons several hours in advance; cover them with cling film and refrigerate until you are ready to cook.

makes 20

prep 20 mins
• cook 10 mins

steamer (bamboo preferred) and wire rack

freeze, uncooked, for up to 1 month

Baked white fish in wine and herbs

You can use any white fish for this dish, such as haddock, pollack, turbot, or sustainable cod.

INGREDIENTS
675g (1½lb) white fish, skinned and cut into 4 pieces
salt
1 large glass of white wine
12 cherry tomatoes
handful of flat-leaf parsley, finely chopped

METHOD
1 Preheat the oven to 190°C (375°F/Gas 5). Sprinkle the fish with salt, then lay in an ovenproof dish. Pour over the wine, and add the tomatoes and parsley.

2 Cover the dish tightly with foil, then bake in the oven for 15–20 minutes, until the fish is cooked through and the alcohol has evaporated.

GOOD WITH A salad and fresh crusty bread for a summery dish, or creamy mashed potatoes for winter.

serves 4

prep 5 mins
• cook 20 mins

healthy option

Couscous with pine nuts and almonds

A tasty alternative to rice; serve either hot or cold.

INGREDIENTS
175g (6oz) couscous
boiling water, to cover
1 red pepper, deseeded and chopped
100g (3½oz) raisins
100g (3½oz) dried apricots, chopped
½ cucumber, seeded and diced
12 black olives, pitted
60g (2oz) blanched almonds, lightly toasted
60g (2oz) pine nuts, lightly toasted
4 tbsp light olive oil
juice of ½ lemon
1 tbsp chopped mint
salt and freshly ground black pepper

METHOD
1 Put the couscous in a bowl and pour over enough boiling water to cover it by about 2.5cm (1in). Set aside for 15 minutes, or until the couscous has absorbed all the water, then fluff the grains up lightly with a fork.

2 Stir in the pepper, raisins, apricots, cucumber, olives, almonds, and pine nuts.

3 Whisk together the olive oil, lemon juice, and mint. Season to taste with salt and pepper and stir into the couscous. Serve at once while warm, or leave to cool.

GOOD WITH Grilled meats, chicken, or fish.

PREPARE AHEAD The couscous can be prepared several hours in advance, if serving cold.

serves 4

prep 15 mins,
plus standing

Vegetable kebabs

Cook these delicious kebabs under the grill or on a barbecue.

INGREDIENTS

1 courgette
1 red pepper, deseeded
1 green pepper, deseeded
1 red onion
8 cherry tomatoes
8 button mushrooms
5 tbsp olive oil
1 garlic clove, crushed
$\frac{1}{2}$ tsp dried oregano
pinch of chilli flakes

METHOD

1 Trim the courgette and cut into 8 chunks. Cut the peppers into 2.5cm (1in) pieces. Peel the onion, and cut into wedges, leaving the root end intact so that the wedges do not fall apart.

2 Thread the vegetables on to 4 large or 8 small skewers. Whisk the remaining ingredients together in a small bowl with a fork to make a flavoured oil.

3 Preheat the grill on a medium-high setting. Place the kebabs on the grill rack and brush generously with the flavoured oil. Cook for 10–15 minutes, or until the vegetables are just tender, turning frequently and brushing with more of the oil as you do so. Drizzle any remaining oil over the cooked kebabs.

GOOD WITH A leafy salad, for a light vegetarian meal.

PREPARE AHEAD Steps 1 and 2 can be completed several hours in advance.

serves 4

prep 15 mins
• cook 15 mins

if using wooden or
bamboo skewers,
soak them for 30
mins before use

4–8 skewers

Egg noodles with lemon and herbs

Fresh Asian noodles absorb the flavours they are cooked in.

INGREDIENTS

2 tbsp vegetable oil
4 spring onions, finely sliced, plus 1 extra,
  finely shredded, to garnish
1 stalk lemongrass, very finely sliced
2.5cm (1in) piece of fresh root ginger,
  peeled and grated
350g (12oz) fresh egg noodles
  or 175g (6oz) dried egg noodles, cooked
2 tbsp light soy sauce
juice of 1 lemon
pinch of sugar
2 tbsp snipped chives
2 tbsp chopped flat-leaf parsley
lemon zest, cut into fine strips, to garnish

METHOD

1 Heat the oil in a wok or large, deep frying pan, add the spring onions, lemongrass, and ginger, and stir-fry for 1 minute.

2 Add the noodles and toss over the heat for 2 minutes. Mix together the soy sauce, lemon juice, and sugar, and pour over the noodles. Stir-fry for a further 2 minutes, or until the noodles are heated through.

3 Sprinkle the chives and parsley over the top, then toss with the noodles and transfer to a serving bowl. Serve at once, garnished with the lemon zest and spring onion.

serves 4

prep 10 mins
• cook 5 mins

healthy option

Pea and mint soup

This soup preserves the fresh taste of its ingredients.

INGREDIENTS

250g (9oz) frozen peas, such as
  petit pois
450ml (15fl oz) hot vegetable stock
handful of mint leaves, roughly chopped
a few thyme stalks, leaves picked
salt and freshly ground black pepper
1–2 tbsp crème fraîche (optional)
pinch of freshly grated nutmeg

METHOD

1 Put the peas in a bowl, pour over boiling water, and leave to stand for about 5 minutes. Drain.

2 Using a blender, process the peas, stock, and herbs until smooth and combined. You may have to do this in batches. Add more stock if the soup is too thick. Season well with salt and pepper, and process again.

3 To serve, stir through the crème fraîche (if using), and top with a pinch of nutmeg. This soup can be served hot or cold.

GOOD WITH Fresh crusty bread.

serves 4

prep 10 mins

healthy option

blender

Spiced orzo with spinach

Orzo is, in fact, a tiny pasta that looks similar to rice. Enjoy on its own or with Mediterranean-style dishes.

INGREDIENTS

200g (7oz) orzo
1½ tbsp olive oil
1 onion, finely chopped
2 garlic cloves, finely chopped
1 tsp ground coriander
½ tsp ground cumin
pinch of cayenne pepper
150g (5½oz) baby spinach leaves
4 tbsp chopped coriander or flat-leaf parsley
salt and freshly ground black pepper

METHOD

1 Bring a large saucepan of salted water to the boil. Add the orzo and cook for 15 minutes, or according to the packet instructions.

2 Meanwhile, heat the olive oil in a large saucepan. Add the onion and fry over a medium heat for 3 minutes, or until just soft but not coloured. Stir in the garlic, coriander, cumin, and cayenne, and continue frying for a further minute.

3 Add the spinach to the pan with the water clinging to its leaves from washing. Cook, stirring, for 3 minutes, or until it is just wilted.

4 Drain the orzo well, shaking off any excess water. Tip the orzo into the pan with spinach and mix the ingredients together, using 2 spoons or forks. Stir in the coriander and season to taste with salt and pepper. Transfer to a serving bowl and serve.

PREPARE AHEAD The whole dish can be made up to 1 day in advance, refrigerated, and served cold. Add extra olive oil and toss, if needed.

serves 4–6

prep 5 mins
• cook 25 mins

healthy option

Kasha pilaf

This is a fragrant and tasty Middle Eastern-style dish.

INGREDIENTS

2 tbsp butter
1 large onion, chopped
2 celery sticks, sliced
1 large egg, lightly beaten
200g (7oz) coarse kasha (buckwheat groats) or whole kasha
1 tsp ground sage
1 tsp ground thyme
115g (4oz) raisins
115g (4oz) walnut pieces, coarsely chopped
salt

METHOD

1 In a large frying pan, melt the butter and gently fry the onion and celery for 3 minutes, or until the vegetables begin to soften.

2 In a small bowl, mix the egg with the kasha, then add the mixture to the pan. Cook, stirring constantly, for 1 minute, or until the grains are dry and separated. Add 500ml (16fl oz) water, the sage, and thyme to the kasha. Bring to the boil, then reduce the heat, cover, and simmer for 10–12 minutes.

3 Stir the raisins and walnuts into the kasha. Cook for a further 4–5 minutes, or until the kasha is tender and all the liquid has been absorbed. Season to taste with salt.

serves 4–6

prep 5 mins
• cook 25 mins

Lentil, broad bean, and feta salad

A healthy, substantial salad that is sure to satisfy any hunger pangs.

INGREDIENTS

85g (3oz) frozen broad beans
400g can green or brown lentils in water, drained and rinsed
salt and freshly ground black pepper
1 bunch of spring onions, finely chopped
1 green chilli, deseeded and finely chopped
175g (6oz) feta cheese, cut into cubes
handful of flat-leaf parsley, finely chopped

For the dressing

3 tbsp olive oil
1 tbsp white wine vinegar
2.5cm (1in) piece of fresh root ginger, peeled and grated
salt and freshly ground black pepper
pinch of caster sugar (optional)

METHOD

1 Soak the broad beans in boiling water for 5 minutes, then drain.

2 Put the lentils in a serving bowl, and season with a pinch of salt and some pepper. Add the spring onions, chilli, and drained broad beans, and stir well.

3 To make the dressing, put the oil, vinegar, and ginger in a jug or small bowl. Season with salt and pepper, and a pinch of sugar (if using), and whisk until well combined. Drizzle over the salad and leave to stand for 10 minutes, to allow the flavours to develop. When ready to serve, stir through the feta and parsley.

serves 4

prep 15 mins

healthy option

Vegetarian Pad Thai

This popular Thai noodle dish is made more substantial by adding tofu.

INGREDIENTS

250g (9oz) wide or medium rice noodles
3–4 tbsp vegetable oil
200g (7oz) firm tofu, cut into cubes
2 garlic cloves, grated or finely chopped
1 egg, lightly beaten
150ml (5fl oz) hot vegetable stock
juice of 1 lime
1 tsp Thai fish sauce, such as nam pla (optional)
2 tsp tamarind paste
2 tsp demerara sugar
1 tbsp dark soy sauce
1 red chilli, deseeded and finely chopped
25g (scant 1oz) dry-roasted peanuts, roughly chopped
1 bunch of spring onions, finely chopped
75g (2$\frac{1}{2}$oz) beansprouts (optional)
small handful of coriander leaves, to garnish

METHOD

1 Soak the rice noodles in boiling water for 10 minutes, then drain. Meanwhile, heat 1 tbsp of the vegetable oil in a wok over a medium-high heat, and swirl it around to coat the surface. Add the tofu, and cook for about 10 minutes until golden. Remove with a slotted spoon, and set aside.

2 Add another tbsp of oil to the pan. When hot, add the garlic and cook for 10 seconds, then tip in the egg and cook, stirring and breaking it up with a wooden spoon, until scrambled. Remove from the pan, and set aside.

3 Add $\frac{1}{2}$ tbsp of the oil. When hot, add the drained noodles, and stir gently to coat with the oil. Pour over the stock, lime juice, fish sauce (if using), tamarind paste, sugar, and soy sauce; toss to combine. Let it simmer for a few minutes, sprinkle over the chilli, and stir through.

4 Add half of the peanuts, the spring onions, and the beansprouts (if using), and stir-fry for a minute. Now add the reserved tofu and scrambled egg, stir to combine, and transfer to a serving plate. Scatter over the remaining peanuts and a sprinkling of coriander leaves to serve.

serves 4

prep 15 mins
• cook 15 mins

healthy option

wok

Linguine alle vongole

Versions of this popular classic of linguine and clams are cooked all along the Italian Mediterranean and Adriatic coasts.

INGREDIENTS

2 tbsp olive oil
1 onion, finely chopped
2 garlic cloves, finely chopped
400g can chopped tomatoes
2 tbsp sun-dried tomato purée
120ml (4fl oz) dry white wine
2 x 140g jars clams in natural juice, strained, with the juice reserved
salt and freshly ground black pepper
350g (12oz) dried linguine
4 tbsp finely chopped flat-leaf parsley, plus extra to garnish

METHOD

1 Heat the oil in a large saucepan over medium heat. Add the onion and garlic and fry, stirring frequently, for 5 minutes or until softened. Add the tomatoes with their juices, tomato purée, wine, and reserved clam juice, and season to taste with salt and pepper, then bring to the boil, stirring. Reduce the heat to low, partially cover the pan, and leave to simmer for 10 minutes or more, stirring occasionally.

2 Meanwhile, bring a large pan of salted water to the boil over a high heat. Add the linguine, stir, and boil for 10 minutes, or until the pasta is cooked but still firm to the bite. Drain the pasta into a large colander and shake to remove any excess water.

3 Add the clams and chopped parsley to the sauce and continue to simmer for a couple of minutes to heat through. Season with salt and pepper to taste.

4 Add the linguine to the sauce and use 2 forks to toss and combine all the ingredients so the pasta is well coated and the clams evenly distributed. Sprinkle with extra parsley and serve at once.

GOOD WITH Crusty Italian bread or a green salad.

serves 4

prep 5 mins
• cook 25 mins

Fettucine Alfredo

A simple supper made with a few good-quality ingredients.

INGREDIENTS

450g (1lb) dried fettucine
115g (4oz) unsalted butter, cubed
250ml (9fl oz) double cream
75g (2½oz) Parmesan cheese, grated,
   plus extra shavings to serve
salt and freshly ground black pepper

METHOD

1 Bring a large saucepan of lightly salted water to the boil, then add the pasta. Simmer for 10–12 minutes or until the pasta is cooked but still firm to the bite. Drain well, return to the pan, and cover to keep warm.

2 In a separate large pan, melt the butter, then add the cream, and heat until hot but not boiling. Reduce the heat to low, add the cooked pasta and the grated Parmesan, and season to taste with pepper. Gently toss the pasta to coat and serve immediately, scattered with Parmesan shavings.

serves 4

prep 5 mins
• cook 15 mins

Rice balls filled with cheese

A great way of using up leftover rice, these little snacks are very satisfying.

INGREDIENTS
225g (8oz) cold cooked Arborio or other risotto rice
pinch of salt
2 balls of fresh mozzarella cheese, cubed
1 egg, beaten
60g (2oz) fresh breadcrumbs, toasted
olive oil, for frying

METHOD
1 Generously season the cold risotto rice with salt, then roll it into 12 even-sized balls.

2 Push a cube of mozzarella into the centre of each ball, then cover so that the cheese is enclosed.

3 Roll each ball first in the beaten egg, then in the toasted breadcrumbs. Heat some olive oil in a frying pan over a medium-high heat, and fry each ball for 2–5 minutes, or until golden.

serves 4

prep 25 mins
• cook 5 mins

Kässpätzle

Spätzle are a type of noodle popular in Switzerland; here they are tossed with eggs and cheese.

INGREDIENTS
400g (14oz) plain flour
1½ tbsp semolina or ground rice
6 eggs
100ml (3½fl oz) milk
½ tsp freshly grated nutmeg
60g (2oz) butter
115g (4oz) Gruyère cheese, grated
freshly ground black pepper
2 spring onions, finely sliced

METHOD
1 Sift the flour into a bowl and stir in the semolina. Lightly beat 4 eggs with the milk, nutmeg, and 100ml (3½fl oz) cold water. Add the egg mixture to the flour, mixing to make a slightly sticky elastic dough, adding more flour, if necessary.

2 Bring a large saucepan of water to the boil. Press the mixture through the holes of a colander (the holes should be medium-sized) over the saucepan, letting the noodles drop into the water. Take care to protect your hands from the steam.

3 Cook for 2–3 minutes, or until the noodles float to the top. Drain and run cold water over to stop them cooking any further. Drain again.

4 Heat the butter in a large frying pan, add the noodles, and toss over a low heat until coated and starting to turn golden. Sprinkle in the cheese; beat the remaining 2 eggs and pour over the spätzle. Season to taste with pepper and cook for 1–2 minutes, or until the cheese melts and the eggs set. Serve with the spring onions scattered over.

serves 4

prep 20 mins
• cook 10 mins

colander
with medium-
sized holes

Tomato bulgur wheat with capers and olives

This dish gives Middle-Eastern bulgur wheat a Mediterranean character.

INGREDIENTS

350g (12oz) bulgur wheat
salt and freshly ground black pepper
150–300ml (5–10fl oz) tomato juice
3 tsp capers in vinegar, drained
12 black olives, pitted and halved
12 green olives, pitted and halved

METHOD

1 Tip the bulgur wheat into a large bowl, then pour over enough boiling water just to cover – about 300ml (10fl oz). Leave to stand for about 15 minutes.

2 Season generously with salt and pepper, and stir well with a fork to fluff up the grains. Add the tomato juice, a little at a time, until the bulgur has absorbed all the juice. Leave to stand for a few minutes between each addition – the bulgur will absorb quite a lot of moisture.

3 Now add the capers and olives, taste, and season again if needed.

GOOD WITH A crisp green salad and some warm pitta bread.

serves 4

prep 15 mins,
plus standing

healthy option

Pasta with sun-dried tomato pesto

Home-made pesto has a wonderful, fresh taste and is very quick to make.

INGREDIENTS

½ 270g jar sun-dried tomatoes in oil, drained
handful of pine nuts
2 garlic cloves, roughly chopped
handful of basil leaves, plus extra leaves to garnish (optional)
50g (1¾oz) Parmesan cheese, grated (more if required)
salt and freshly ground black pepper
extra virgin olive oil
350g (12oz) dried fusilli

METHOD

1 Place the first five ingredients in a food processor and whiz until blended. Season with salt and pepper and whiz again. Taste and add more Parmesan and/or some extra virgin olive oil, if required.

2 Cook the pasta in a large pan of boiling salted water for 10 minutes, or until it is cooked but still firm to the bite. Drain, keeping back a tiny amount of the cooking water. Return the pasta to the pan and toss together. Toss with the sauce, drizzle with extra virgin olive oil, garnish with basil leaves (if using), and serve.

PREPARE AHEAD The pesto can be made several days in advance. Spoon it into a jar and top with a thin layer of olive oil – it will keep in the refrigerator for up to 1 week.

serves 4

prep 10 mins
• cook 10 mins

food processor

Tuna and white beans with olives

A speedy no-cook dish with clean, Mediterranean flavours.

INGREDIENTS

400g can butterbeans, drained and rinsed
400g can cannellini beans, drained and rinsed
2 x 200g cans tuna in olive oil, drained
2 tbsp white wine vinegar
salt and freshly ground black pepper
1 tsp wholegrain mustard
$\frac{1}{2}$ tsp mild paprika
about 12 black olives, pitted and halved
2 tsp capers in vinegar, drained

METHOD

1 Tip the beans into a large bowl along with the tuna. Add the vinegar, taste, and season well with salt and pepper.

2 Add the remaining ingredients, and stir through thoroughly. Taste, and season again if needed. Serve immediately.

PREPARE AHEAD The completed dish can be refrigerated for a couple of hours until needed. Bring back to room temperature before serving.

serves 4

prep 10 mins

healthy option

Pasta with pecorino and peas

Pecorino's bold, salty flavour adds character to a simple sauce; if you don't have it, Parmesan works well – just use a little less.

INGREDIENTS
1 tbsp olive oil
1 onion, finely chopped
salt and freshly ground black pepper
1 garlic clove, grated or finely chopped
1 red chilli, deseeded and finely chopped
2 tsp plain flour
½ small glass of dry white wine
150ml (5fl oz) milk
150g (5½oz) frozen peas
125g (4½oz) pecorino cheese,
   grated, plus extra to serve
350g (12oz) dried farfalle pasta

METHOD
1 Heat the oil in a large frying pan, add the onion and a pinch of salt, and cook over a low heat for 5 minutes, or until soft and translucent. Stir in the garlic and chilli and cook for a few seconds more. Stir in the flour, then add the wine, and simmer for a couple of minutes. Add the milk and stir.

2 Stir in the peas, then add the pecorino, and cook at a low simmer – do not allow to boil – for 10 minutes or until the sauce has thickened slightly. Season well with salt and pepper.

3 Meanwhile, cook the pasta in a pan of boiling salted water for 10 minutes, or until it is cooked but still firm to the bite. Drain, keeping back a tiny amount of the cooking water. Return the pasta to the pan and toss together. Toss with the sauce, top with extra pecorino, and serve.

serves 4

prep 10 mins
• cook 20 mins

Lentils with artichokes and peppers

Juicy, crunchy, salty, and sweet – this quick, filling salad has it all.

INGREDIENTS

400g can Puy lentils, drained and rinsed
400g can artichoke hearts, drained and sliced
4 or 5 ready-roasted peppers from a jar or the deli counter
1–2 thyme sprigs, leaves only
handful of flat-leaf parsley, finely chopped
4 spring onions, finely chopped
2–3 tbsp walnut oil
1 tbsp cider vinegar
salt and freshly ground black pepper
4 or 5 slices of Parma ham, chopped
handful of wild rocket leaves

METHOD

1 Put the lentils, artichokes, peppers, herbs, and spring onions in a large bowl. Drizzle over the oil and vinegar, season with salt and pepper, and stir well to combine.

2 Add the Parma ham and rocket, toss gently, and transfer to a serving dish.

serves 4

prep 15 mins

healthy option

108

Gnocchi with Gorgonzola and walnut sauce

Blue cheese and walnuts are a classic pairing and make this Italian dish rather special.

INGREDIENTS
knob of butter
1 onion, finely chopped
75g (2½oz) walnuts, roughly chopped
1 tbsp plain flour
450ml (15fl oz) milk
125g (4½oz) Gorgonzola cheese
salt and freshly ground black pepper
500g packet ready-made gnocchi
handful of basil leaves, to garnish (optional)

METHOD
1 In a pan, melt the butter over a low heat. Add the onion, and sweat gently for about 5 minutes until soft and translucent. Now add the walnuts, and cook for another couple of minutes. Remove from the heat, and stir in the flour, then add a little milk. Return to the heat, and add the remaining milk, stirring constantly for 4–6 minutes until the sauce thickens.

2 Remove from the heat again, and stir through the Gorgonzola. Season with salt and pepper.

3 In a separate pan, cook the gnocchi in plenty of boiling salted water for a few minutes, or according to the packet instructions. Drain well. Add to the sauce, and stir through well. Garnish with the basil leaves (if using), and serve immediately.

GOOD WITH A tomato and rocket salad.

serves 4

prep 10 mins
• cook 20 mins

Egg fu yung

Light and tasty Chinese patties made with prawns and stir-fried vegetables.

INGREDIENTS

200ml (7fl oz) vegetable stock
1 tbsp oyster sauce
1 tbsp light soy sauce
1 tbsp Chinese rice wine
vegetable oil, for frying
3 shallots, thinly sliced
2 garlic cloves, crushed
1 green pepper, deseeded and chopped
1 celery stick, chopped
85g (3oz) beansprouts
115g (4oz) frozen prawns, thawed
5 eggs, beaten
2 tsp cornflour
boiled rice, to serve

METHOD

1 In a small saucepan, add the stock, oyster sauce, soy sauce, and rice wine. Set aside.

2 Heat 2 tbsp oil in a wok and stir-fry the shallots, garlic, green pepper, and celery for 3 minutes. Add the beansprouts and stir-fry for 2 minutes. Then add the prawns, and stir-fry for 1 minute more. Transfer to a large bowl and set aside.

3 When the mixture is cool, stir in the beaten eggs. Wipe the pan with kitchen paper.

4 Return the wok to the heat and pour in 5cm (2in) oil. When hot, ladle $^1/_4$ of the mixture into the oil and fry for 2 minutes, or until lightly browned, spooning over the oil so the top starts to set as well.

5 Carefully turn over and cook the other side. Drain and keep warm. Cook the rest of the mixture.

6 Mix the cornflour with a little water until smooth and stir into the stock mixture in the saucepan. Bring to the boil, stirring constantly until thickened and smooth, and simmer for 1 minute. Spoon over the egg fu yung patties and serve at once with boiled rice.

serves 4

prep 15 mins
• cook 20 mins

wok

Bean burgers

A tasty and low-fat alternative to burgers made with meat.

INGREDIENTS

400g can aduki beans, drained and rinsed
400g can chickpeas, drained and rinsed
1 onion, roughly chopped
6 salted anchovies in olive oil, drained
1 tbsp wholegrain mustard
salt and freshly ground black pepper
2 eggs
2–3 tbsp plain flour, plus extra for dusting
2–3 tbsp vegetable or sunflower oil, for frying

METHOD

1 Put the drained beans and chickpeas in a food processor, and pulse several times until the beans are broken up.

2 Add the onion, anchovies, and mustard to the food processor, and season well with salt and pepper. Pulse again a few times. You want the mixture to be well combined, but not sloppy. Now add the eggs, and pulse again until combined. Add the flour (just enough to bind the burgers), and pulse until incorporated.

3 Heat 1 tsp oil in a large non-stick frying pan over a medium heat. Once the oil is hot, spoon out a portion of the bean mixture (it makes 6 burgers) and, using lots of flour on your hands, form into a flattened burger before adding to the pan. Fry undisturbed for 2–3 minutes on each side until firm and golden. Cook in batches of 2 or 3 burgers at a time, forming the burgers as you go, and adding more oil when needed. Serve hot.

GOOD WITH A toasted burger bun, crisp lettuce, and tomato ketchup.

serves 6

prep 15 mins
• cook 10 mins

healthy option

food processor

freeze, uncooked,
for up to 1 month

Paneer and peas

Called *matar paneer* on Indian restaurant menus, this is easy to make at home.

INGREDIENTS

groundnut oil or sunflower oil for frying
1 large onion, thinly sliced
2 large garlic cloves, coarsely chopped
1 green chilli, deseeded (optional) and chopped
1cm (1/2in) fresh root ginger, peeled and coarsely chopped
2 tsp garam masala
salt and freshly ground black pepper
400g can chopped tomatoes
225g (8oz) paneer, cut into bite-sized cubes
450g (1lb) frozen peas

METHOD

1 Heat a large, heavy frying pan over a medium heat. Add 3 tbsp of the oil. When the oil is hot, fry the onion, stirring frequently, for 8–10 minutes, or until dark golden brown. Do not let the onion burn.

2 Meanwhile, put the garlic, chilli, and ginger into a blender, and blend until a thick paste forms. Add the garam masala and season with salt and pepper.

3 Add the spice mixture to the fried onions and stir for a couple of minutes. Pour into a large, heavy saucepan, add the tomatoes and 150ml (5fl oz) water, and bring to the boil, stirring. Reduce the heat to low and leave to simmer and thicken while preparing the paneer, stirring.

4 Wash and dry the frying pan and place over a high heat. When the pan is hot, pour a thin layer of oil over the surface. Once hot, add as many pieces of paneer that will fit in a single layer and fry for 5 minutes, or until golden on all sides, using long-handled tongs to turn them. As the pieces are fried, transfer them into the simmering tomato mixture.

5 When all the paneer has been transferred, add the frozen peas to the saucepan, increase the heat and leave to cook for 5 minutes, or until the peas are cooked. Stir carefully to avoid breaking up the paneer. Taste and adjust the seasoning, if necessary.

GOOD WITH Hot chapatis.

serves 4

prep 10 mins
• cook 25 mins

blender

116

Pasta with olives, capers, and sun-dried tomatoes

Preserved ingredients have deeper, more intense flavours, as well as being convenient.

INGREDIENTS

350g (12oz) dried penne or other dried pasta of your choice
1 tbsp olive oil
3 tsp salted capers, rinsed and gently squeezed dry
handful of black olives, pitted
6 sun-dried tomatoes in oil, chopped
   (reserve a little of the oil, optional)
salt and freshly ground black pepper

METHOD

1 Cook the pasta in a pan of boiling salted water for 8–10 minutes, or according to the packet instructions, until firm to the bite. Drain, and return to the pan with a little of the cooking water.

2 Meanwhile, in another pan, heat the olive oil over a low heat. Add the capers, olives, and sun-dried tomatoes, and cook gently for about 5 minutes, squashing them slightly with the back of a fork.

3 Tip the mixture over the cooked pasta, and toss through until evenly mixed. Add a little of the reserved oil from the sun-dried tomatoes (if using). Season well with salt and pepper, and serve immediately.

serves 4

prep 10 mins
• cook 15 mins

Welsh rarebit

Often pronounced as Welsh "rabbit", this simple recipe makes a meal out of cheese on toast.

INGREDIENTS

4 slices of white bread or wholemeal bread
25g (scant 1oz) butter
225g (8oz) strong Cheddar cheese
   or Lancashire cheese, grated
1 tbsp English mustard powder
3 tbsp brown ale or lager
Worcestershire sauce, to taste

METHOD

1 Preheat the grill to high and position the rack 10cm (4in) from the heat. Toast the bread until golden brown, then turn over, and toast the other side. Leaving the grill on, remove the toast from the heat, and place on to a baking tray.

2 Meanwhile, melt the butter in a pan over a low heat. Add the cheese, mustard powder, and ale, and heat until creamy, stirring often.

3 Spread the sauce over the toast and splash a few drops of Worcestershire sauce on each. Return the cheese-covered toast to the grill for just a few minutes, or until the cheese is bubbling and golden. Cut each slice in half and serve.

GOOD WITH A fresh watercress and tomato salad.

serves 4

**prep 10 mins
• cook 6 mins**

**line the baking
tray with kitchen
foil before baking,
as the cheese
sauce will be hot
and runny**

Rice and beans

Coconut and chillies give this Caribbean-inspired dish a rich, spicy flavour.

INGREDIENTS
1 tbsp olive oil
1 onion, finely chopped
2 garlic cloves, grated or finely chopped
2–3 red chillies, deseeded and finely chopped
450g (1lb) basmati rice, rinsed
400g can black-eye beans, drained and rinsed
400g can coconut milk
500ml (16fl oz) hot vegetable stock
salt and freshly ground black pepper

METHOD
1 Heat the oil in a large lidded pan over a low heat, and sweat the onion for 5 minutes until soft and translucent. Add the garlic and chillies, and cook for a few seconds more.

2 Stir through the rice, making sure that the grains are well coated, then tip in the beans, coconut milk, and most of the stock. Cover the pan, and gently cook over a low heat for about 20 minutes until all the liquid has been absorbed and the rice is cooked; if you need to add more stock, do so.

3 Season to taste with salt and pepper, and serve hot.

GOOD WITH Freshly steamed, boiled, or sautéed vegetables.

serves 4

prep 5 mins
• cook 25 mins

healthy option

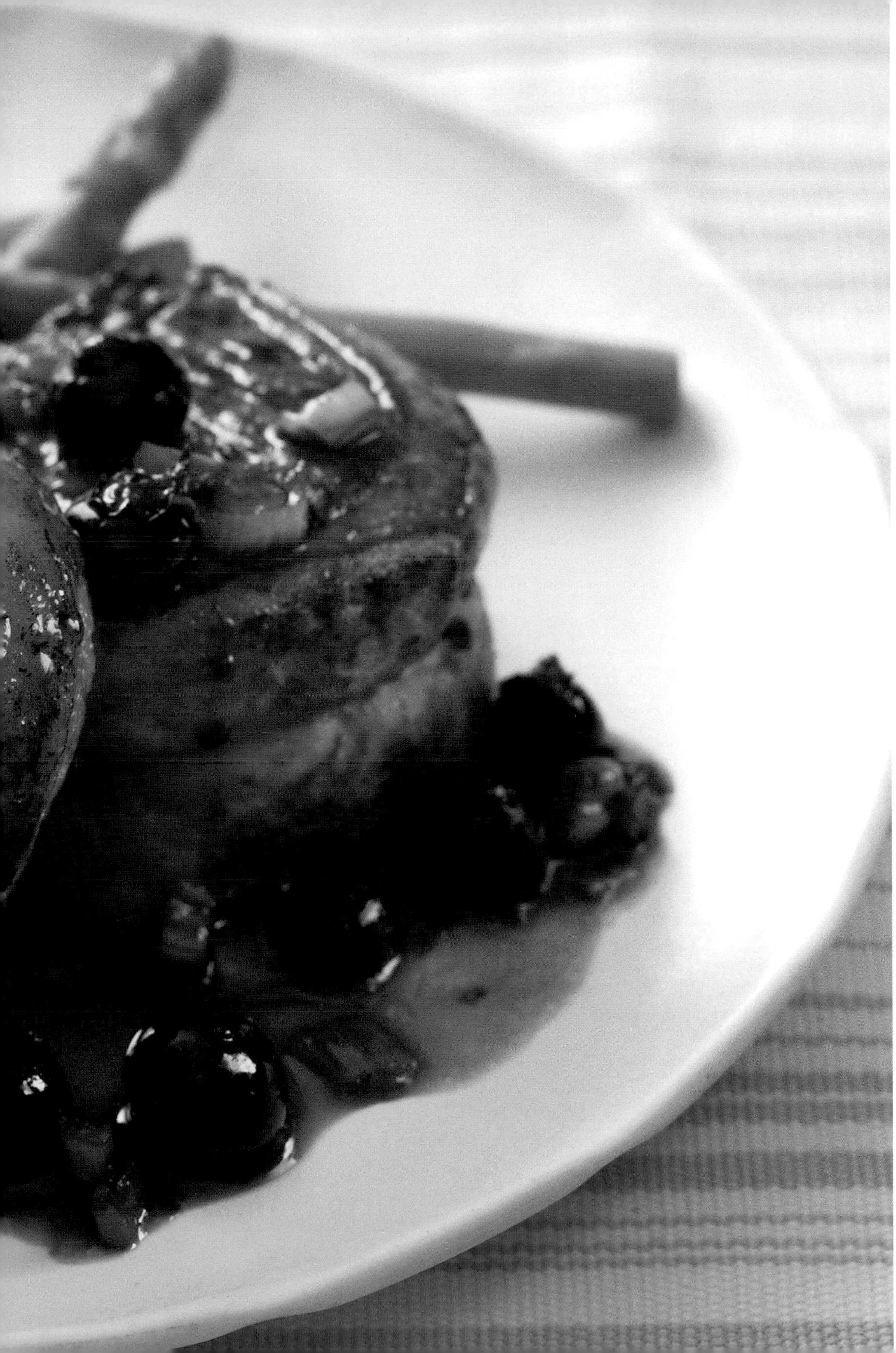

HEARTY AND FILLING

Lamb koftas

Tender minced lamb kebabs with a hint of Middle-Eastern spices.

INGREDIENTS

1 slice of white bread, crusts removed and torn into small pieces
3 tbsp milk
450g (1lb) minced lamb
8 sprigs of coriander, leaves finely chopped
8 sprigs of parsley, leaves finely chopped
1 tbsp ground cumin
1 garlic clove, crushed
½ tsp salt
½ tsp freshly ground black pepper
vegetable oil, for brushing

For the sauce

115g (4oz) cucumber, deseeded and diced
300g (10oz) plain yogurt

METHOD

1 Soak the bread in the milk for 5 minutes.

2 Put the minced lamb, coriander, parsley, cumin, garlic, salt, and pepper in a large bowl. Squeeze the milk from the bread and add the bread to the bowl. Mix thoroughly with your hands. Discard the remaining milk.

3 Using wet hands, roll 2 tbsp of the mixture into an even round shape, then repeat with the remaining mixture to make a total of 16 koftas. Carefully skewer each kofta with a skewer.

4 Meanwhile, preheat the grill on its highest setting. Line the grill pan with kitchen foil and lightly brush the grill rack with vegetable oil. Position the rack about 10cm (4in) from the heat.

5 Put the koftas on a grill rack in the grill pan and grill, turning frequently, for 8 minutes for slightly pink, or 10 minutes for well done. Mix the cucumber and yogurt with a little salt to taste and serve alongside the cooked koftas.

GOOD WITH Pitta bread.

PREPARE AHEAD Steps 1, 2, and 3 can be completed up to a day in advance; keep the uncooked koftas chilled. The sauce can be made up to 2 days in advance, but if left too long it will become watery.

makes 16

**prep 15 mins,
plus soaking
• cook 8–10 mins**

**if using wooden
or bamboo
skewers,
soak them
for 30 mins
before use**

16 skewers

Chicken fajitas with tomato and avocado salsa

This speedy version of the Mexican favourite uses clever short-cuts to achieve the flavours of the original.

INGREDIENTS

1 tbsp olive oil
2 onions, sliced into strips
2 red peppers, deseeded and cut
   into strips
2 green peppers, deseeded and cut
   into strips
2 red chillies, deseeded and finely chopped
2 garlic cloves, sliced
4 skinless chicken breast fillets,
   cut into strips
1 small glass of dry white wine
handful of coriander leaves,
   finely chopped
12 corn tortillas

For the salsa

1 ripe avocado
handful of cherry tomatoes, chopped
1 bunch of spring onions,
   finely chopped
handful of flat-leaf parsley, finely chopped
1 tbsp olive oil
1 tbsp white wine vinegar
salt and freshly ground black pepper

METHOD

1 First, make the salsa. Halve, stone, peel, and chop the avocado. Put in a bowl with the tomatoes, spring onions, and parsley. Drizzle over the olive oil and vinegar. Season with salt and pepper.

2 To make the chicken fajitas, heat the oil in a large frying pan over a low heat. Add the onions and red and green peppers, and sauté for 5 minutes until starting to soften. Stir through the chilli and garlic, and cook for a few seconds.

3 Increase the heat to medium-high, and add the chicken. Keep the mixture moving around the pan, so that it doesn't burn and the chicken is evenly cooked. Stir-fry for 3–5 minutes until the chicken is no longer pink. Pour in the wine, and cook fiercely for 5 minutes. Stir through the coriander.

4 To serve, spoon the mixture on to the tortillas. Top with the salsa, and roll into wraps. Serve any extra salsa on the side.

GOOD WITH Soured cream as an extra sauce.

serves 4

prep 15 mins
• cook 15 mins

Frikadeller

This is a Danish classic, made here with chicken instead of veal.

INGREDIENTS

250g (9oz) minced pork
250g (9oz) minced chicken or turkey
1 onion, grated
60g (2oz) fresh white breadcrumbs
5–6 tbsp milk
1/2 tsp dried thyme
salt and freshly ground black pepper
1 egg, beaten
flour, for dusting
sunflower oil, for shallow frying
1 lemon, cut into wedges, to serve

METHOD

1 Put the pork, chicken, onion, breadcrumbs, milk, and thyme in a large bowl. Mix together and season with salt and pepper.

2 Stir in the egg and a little extra milk, if necessary, to make the mixture soft but not sticky. With lightly floured hands, shape the mixture into 16 small balls.

3 Heat the oil in a frying pan and fry the meatballs over a medium heat for 8–10 minutes, turning often, until golden brown.

4 Drain on kitchen paper, then serve while still hot, with lemon wedges.

serves 4

prep 15 mins
• cook 10 mins

freeze the
meatballs, raw or
cooked, for up to
3 months

Pork chops with green peppercorn sauce

These soft, mild peppercorns add a gentle spice to the creamy sauce.

INGREDIENTS

4 lean pork loin chops
salt and freshly ground black pepper
1 tbsp sunflower oil

For the sauce

30g (1oz) butter
1 large shallot, finely chopped
4 tbsp dry sherry
1$\frac{1}{2}$ tbsp green peppercorns in brine, rinsed,
   drained, and lightly crushed
150ml (5fl oz) chicken stock
4 tbsp crème fraîche

METHOD

1 Trim the chops of excess fat and season with salt and pepper. Heat the oil in a large, heavy frying pan on medium heat and fry the chops for 6–8 minutes on each side, depending on thickness, until golden brown and the juices run clear. Remove from the pan to a warm plate and cover with foil.

2 Meanwhile, make the sauce. Melt the butter in the pan and fry the shallot over medium heat for 4–5 minutes, stirring often, until soft but not browned. Stir in the sherry and simmer for about 1 minute. Add the peppercorns and stock, bring to the boil, and simmer for 2–3 minutes, or until slightly reduced.

3 Stir in the crème fraîche, spoon the sauce over the chops, and serve immediately.

GOOD WITH Potato rösti cakes and steamed green vegetables.

serves 4

prep 10 mins
• cook 15 mins

Kidneys with mustard sauce

This dish makes a tasty and wholesome supper.

INGREDIENTS
4 lamb's kidneys
30g (1oz) butter
1 tbsp olive oil
1 large onion, finely chopped
2 garlic cloves, crushed
8 chestnut mushrooms, sliced
3 tbsp vermouth or red wine
4 tbsp vegetable stock
2 tsp Dijon mustard
salt and freshly ground black pepper

METHOD
1 Peel away any skin from the kidneys and cut out the core and membranes. Soak for 5–10 minutes in a little milk or water, then drain, and pat dry on kitchen paper.

2 Heat the butter and oil in a frying pan, add the onion, and fry over a medium heat, stirring frequently, for 2–3 minutes. Increase the heat, add the kidneys and garlic, and fry for 2–3 minutes, stirring.

3 Add the mushrooms, fry for a further 2–3 minutes, then add the vermouth or red wine and the stock, and allow to bubble for 1 minute.

4 Reduce the heat, cover, and cook for 4 minutes, or until the kidneys are tender and cooked through. Stir in the mustard and season to taste with salt and pepper.

GOOD WITH Slices of toasted wholemeal bread.

serves 4

prep 10 mins,
plus soaking
• cook 10–15 mins

Lamb with blueberries

Blueberries and fresh mint offset the richness of lamb.

INGREDIENTS

8–12 noisettes of lamb
salt and freshly ground black pepper
2 tbsp olive oil
3 spring onions, chopped
1½ tbsp redcurrant jelly
150ml (5fl oz) lamb stock
150g (5½oz) blueberries
2 tbsp finely chopped mint

METHOD

1 Season the lamb noisettes with salt and pepper. Heat half the oil in a large, heavy frying pan and fry the noisettes for 4–6 minutes on each side, or until golden brown but still slightly pink inside. Remove on to a plate and cover with foil.

2 Add the remaining oil to the pan and fry the onions for 2–3 minutes, then stir in the redcurrant jelly and stock. Stir until the jelly is dissolved and the liquid comes to the boil.

3 Add the blueberries and simmer, uncovered, for 2 minutes, then add the mint.

4 Serve the lamb with the sauce spooned over.

serves 4

prep 10 mins
• cook 8–12 mins

Wasabi beef and pak choi

Similar in taste to horseradish, wasabi is popular in Japanese cooking, and is superb with beef.

INGREDIENTS

2 tbsp olive oil
2 tsp wasabi paste
4 sirloin steaks, about 200g (7oz) each
200g (7oz) pak choi, cut lengthways into 8 pieces
5 garlic cloves, grated or finely chopped
1 tbsp dark soy sauce
salt and freshly ground black pepper

METHOD

1 Heat a ridged cast-iron grill pan until hot. Mix together 1 tbsp of the olive oil and the wasabi paste. Use to coat the sirloin steaks, ensuring a thin, even covering.

2 Sit the steaks on the grill pan and grill fiercely over a high heat for 3 minutes on each side. Remove to a plate, and leave to rest in a warm place for 5 minutes.

3 Meanwhile, toss the pak choi in the remaining olive oil with the garlic and soy sauce. Grill for 2–3 minutes, or until charred and just wilted. To serve, cut the steak into 1cm (½in) slices, season, and serve with the pak choi.

serves 4

prep 10 mins
• cook 10 mins

ridged cast-iron
grill pan

Mussels in fennel broth

This fragrant broth with coconut and juicy mussels makes an impressive dish.

INGREDIENTS
1 tbsp olive oil
1 onion, finely chopped
1 fennel bulb, trimmed and finely chopped
salt and freshly ground black pepper
2 garlic cloves, grated or finely chopped
2 waxy potatoes, peeled and finely diced
300ml (10fl oz) hot vegetable stock or light fish stock
400g can coconut milk
1.35kg (3lb) fresh mussels, scrubbed and debearded
handful of basil leaves, torn

METHOD
1 Heat the oil in a large pan over a low heat. Add the onion, fennel, and a pinch of salt, then sweat for about 5 minutes until softened. Add the garlic and potatoes, and cook for a few minutes more, being careful not to allow the mixture to brown at all.

2 Pour in the stock, and bring to the boil. Add the coconut milk, reduce the heat slightly, and simmer gently for about 10 minutes, or until the potatoes are cooked. Bring back to the boil, add the mussels, and put a lid on the pan. Cook for about 5 minutes, until all the mussels are open (discard any that do not).

3 To serve, stir through the basil, taste the broth, and season if needed. Serve immediately.

GOOD WITH Fresh crusty bread to mop up the broth.

serves 4

prep 10 mins
• cook 20 mins

before cooking,
tap the mussels
and discard any
that do not close

Black pudding with apple

Sweet apples are the perfect partner for savoury, peppery black pudding and bacon.

INGREDIENTS

3 sweet eating apples, peeled, cored, and sliced
30g (1oz) butter
2 tsp light soft brown sugar
vegetable oil, for frying
8 large slices or 16 small slices of black pudding
4 smoked streaky bacon rashers, cut lengthways into thin strips
100ml (3½fl oz) cider

METHOD

1 Cut each apple slice in half. Melt the butter in a small frying pan, add the apple pieces and sugar, and cook over a medium heat, stirring frequently, for 8–10 minutes, or until softened and slightly caramelized. Remove from the heat and set aside.

2 Wipe out the pan, smear it with a little oil and fry the black pudding slices, in batches, over a medium-high heat for about 3 minutes on each side, or until slightly crisp. Remove from the pan and keep warm. Fry the bacon strips for 3 minutes, or until cooked through and slightly crisp, stirring frequently. Remove from the pan, increase the heat, and pour in the cider. Allow to bubble until well reduced and syrupy, stirring to incorporate any bits stuck to the bottom of the pan.

3 To serve, place a slice of black pudding on each plate, add a layer of apples, then repeat with the rest of the black pudding and apple. Top with the bacon strips and drizzle with the pan juices.

GOOD WITH Creamy mashed potato.

serves 4

prep 10 mins
• cook 20 mins

Baked plaice with bacon

This is a tasty and unusual way of cooking flat fish.

INGREDIENTS

2 tbsp olive oil
4 back bacon rashers, chopped
3 spring onions, chopped
4 plaice fillets, about 175g (6oz) each
freshly ground black pepper
60g (2oz) butter
juice of 1/2 large lemon
1 tbsp chopped parsley

METHOD

1 Preheat the oven to 200°C (400°F/Gas 6). Heat the oil in a roasting tin over medium heat, add the bacon and spring onions, and fry for 2 minutes, stirring frequently.

2 Add the plaice, skin-side down, baste with the oil, and season to taste with pepper.

3 Place the tin in the oven and bake the fish for 15 minutes, basting once or twice.

4 Transfer the cooked plaice to warmed serving plates. Drain the bacon and spring onions from the tin, and set aside.

5 Heat the butter in a small saucepan until golden brown, add the lemon juice, bacon, and onions, and stir in the parsley. Spoon over the plaice and serve at once.

GOOD WITH Stir-fried or steamed vegetables, such as spinach, green beans, or carrots.

serves 4

prep 10 mins
• cook 20 mins

healthy option

Minced chicken with exotic mushrooms, soy, and lime

Bring a taste of the Orient to your table with this easy dish.

INGREDIENTS

2 or 3 skinless chicken breast fillets, roughly sliced
1 tbsp olive oil
1 onion, finely chopped
salt and freshly ground black pepper
1 garlic clove, grated or finely chopped
1 red chilli, deseeded and finely chopped
300g (10oz) mixed fresh exotic mushrooms (such as oyster,
    shiitake, and enoki) or chestnut mushrooms, finely chopped
3 tbsp dark soy sauce
juice of 2 limes
handful of coriander leaves, finely chopped
handful of basil leaves, finely chopped
hot cooked rice, to serve

METHOD

1 Whiz the sliced chicken in a food processor until minced. Set aside.

2 Heat the oil in a large frying pan over a medium heat. Add the onion and a pinch of salt, and sauté for 5 minutes until soft. Add the garlic and chilli, and cook for a few seconds more.

3 Add the chicken mince to the pan, season well with salt and pepper, and cook, stirring occasionally, for a few minutes until the chicken is no longer pink. Add the mushrooms, and cook for about 5 minutes more.

4 Stir through the soy sauce and lime juice, and cook for a further 2 minutes. Taste, and season again if needed. Just before serving, stir through the coriander and basil. Serve immediately with the hot rice, either on the side or mixed together.

serves 4

prep 10 mins
• cook 20 mins

food processor

Bulgur wheat with mixed peppers, mint, and goat's cheese

Sweet, crunchy peppers and creamy goat's cheese are a winning combination.

INGREDIENTS
250g (9oz) fine bulgur wheat
300ml (10fl oz) hot light or low-salt vegetable stock
salt and freshly ground black pepper
1 bunch of spring onions, finely chopped
1 orange pepper, deseeded and diced
1 yellow pepper, deseeded and diced
pinch of mild paprika
handful of fresh mint leaves, finely chopped
juice of 1 lemon
125g (4½oz) soft goat's cheese, crumbled
extra virgin olive oil, for drizzling

METHOD
1 Put the bulgur wheat in a large bowl, and pour over the stock – it should just cover the bulgur. Leave to stand for 10 minutes, then stir with a fork to fluff up the grains. Season well with a pinch of salt and pepper.

2 Add the spring onions, orange and yellow peppers, paprika, mint, and lemon juice, and stir well. Taste, and season again if needed. To serve, top with the goat's cheese and a generous drizzle of olive oil.

serves 4

prep 15 mins

healthy option

Asparagus, broccoli, ginger, and mint stir-fry

Take care not to overcook the vegetables – they should remain crunchy and fresh-tasting.

INGREDIENTS

1 tbsp sesame oil or vegetable oil
2 red chillies, deseeded and finely chopped
5cm (2in) piece of fresh root ginger, sliced into fine strips
1 bunch of spring onions, cut into 5cm (2in) lengths
2 garlic cloves, grated or finely chopped
1 red pepper, deseeded and sliced into fine strips
1 head broccoli, about 300g (10oz), cut into florets
1 bunch of fine asparagus spears, trimmed and halved
1 tbsp caster sugar
salt and freshly ground black pepper
handful of mint leaves

METHOD

1 Heat the oil in a wok over a medium-high heat, and swirl to coat the surface. Add the chillies and ginger and toss for a few seconds, then add the spring onions, and a few seconds later add the garlic. Stir-fry for 5 minutes until soft.

2 Add the pepper, and stir-fry for a few minutes. Add the broccoli, and stir-fry for a few minutes more, before adding the asparagus. Continue stir-frying for another minute or two.

3 Sprinkle the sugar over the vegetables, and season well with salt and pepper. Stir-fry for a few seconds until the sugar has dissolved. Remove from the heat, and stir through the mint leaves. Serve immediately.

GOOD WITH Hot, fluffy rice.

serves 4

prep 15 mins
• cook 15 mins

healthy option

wok

Chargrilled lamb cutlets and aubergine with red cabbage slaw

A range of cooked and raw vegetables provides an array of flavours to complement the simplicity of the lamb.

INGREDIENTS

1 aubergine, about 300g (10oz), thinly sliced lengthways
salt, for sprinkling
12 lamb cutlets, trimmed of any fat
2 tbsp olive oil
salt and freshly ground black pepper

For the red cabbage slaw

½ small red cabbage
100g (3½oz) green beans, trimmed, blanched,
    and thinly sliced diagonally
1 small cucumber, thinly sliced or shaved lengthways
1 spring onion, thinly sliced diagonally
1 small red onion, thinly sliced into discs
2 celery sticks, peeled and thinly sliced diagonally
60g (2oz) hazelnuts, chopped
2 tbsp extra virgin olive oil
1 tsp balsamic vinegar

METHOD

1 Put the aubergine slices in a colander, and sprinkle with salt. Leave to drain for 20 minutes, rinse, and pat dry with kitchen paper.

2 Heat the ridged cast-iron grill pan until hot. Brush the lamb cutlets with olive oil, and season with salt and pepper. Brush the aubergine slices with a little olive oil, and season with pepper. Grill the lamb over a medium heat for 3–5 minutes on each side until cooked to your liking. At the same time, grill the aubergine over a high heat for about 3 minutes on each side until golden. Remove both the lamb and aubergine to a plate, and leave to rest in a warm place for 10 minutes.

3 Meanwhile, finely slice or shred the red cabbage. Put the cabbage in a bowl, and add the remaining slaw ingredients. Season with salt and pepper, toss gently, and serve with the lamb cutlets and chargrilled aubergine.

serves 4

prep 25 mins
• cook 10 mins

ridged cast-iron grill pan

Seared tuna with cucumber and fennel

This tuna is served very rare, so use the freshest possible fish.

INGREDIENTS

6 tbsp olive oil, plus extra for brushing
4 tuna steaks, about 150g (5½oz) each
salt and freshly ground black pepper
1 fennel bulb, sliced
2 shallots, finely chopped
1 cucumber, deseeded, skinned, and finely chopped
30g (1oz) mint, parsley, and chervil leaves, torn and mixed
juice of 1 lemon
8 anchovy fillets
4 lemon wedges, to serve

METHOD

1 Rub 2 tbsp oil over the tuna steaks and sprinkle with lots of pepper. Set aside.

2 Heat 2 tbsp olive oil and sauté the fennel for 4–5 minutes, or until just tender.
Season with salt and pepper. Tip the fennel into a large bowl and set aside to cool a little.

3 Add the shallots, cucumber, and herbs to the fennel. Stir in the lemon juice and remaining oil.

4 Heat a heavy frying pan or grill pan until smoking. Lightly brush the tuna steaks with oil, then pan-fry for 30 seconds. Brush the top with a little more oil, turn over, and cook for a further 30 seconds.

5 Place a tuna steak on each serving plate, with the salad piled on top, and 2 anchovies draped over. Drizzle with the remaining lemon and oil from the bowl, and serve with a wedge of lemon.

GOOD WITH A salad of warm parsley-buttered new potatoes.

serves 4

prep 15 mins,
plus cooling
• cook 6 mins

Tomato and harissa tart

Harissa paste gives this tart a fiery kick.

INGREDIENTS

400g (14oz) ready-made puff pastry
flour, for dusting
2 tbsp red pepper pesto
6 tomatoes, halved
2–3 tbsp harissa paste
1 tbsp olive oil
few sprigs of fresh thyme,
 leaves picked

METHOD

1 Preheat the oven to 200°C (400°F/Gas 6). Roll out the pastry on a floured work surface, into a large rectangle or square. Lay on a baking tray, then use a sharp knife to score a border about 5cm (2in) in from the edges all the way around, being careful not to cut all the way through the pastry. Then use the back of the knife to score the pastry around the outer edges – this will help it to puff up.

2 Working inside the border, smother the pastry with the pesto. Arrange the tomatoes on top, cut-side up. Mix the harissa with the olive oil, and drizzle over the tomatoes. Scatter over the thyme leaves.

3 Bake in the oven for about 15 minutes until the pastry is cooked and golden. Serve hot.

serves 6

prep 10 mins
• cook 15 mins

Chinese-style steamed bass

This impressive restaurant-style dish is surprisingly easy to prepare.

INGREDIENTS
4 tbsp soy sauce
4 tbsp Chinese rice wine or dry sherry
3 tbsp thinly sliced fresh root ginger
2 small sea bass, gutted and rinsed
1 tbsp sesame oil
$^1/_2$ tsp salt
2 spring onions, trimmed and thinly sliced
4 tbsp sunflower oil
2 garlic cloves, chopped
1 small red chillies, deseeded and thinly sliced
thinly sliced zest of 1 limes

METHOD
1 Prepare a steamer, or position a steaming rack in a wok with water so it doesn't touch the water. Bring to the boil.

2 Stir together the soy sauce, rice wine, and 2 tbsp of ginger, and set aside. Using a sharp knife, make slashes in the fish, 2.5cm (1in) apart and not quite as deep as the bone, on both sides. Rub the fish inside and out with the sesame oil and salt.

3 Scatter $^1/_4$ of the spring onions over a heatproof serving dish that will hold 2 fish and fit in the steamer or on the steaming rack. Place the fish on the dish and pour the sauce over.

4 Place the dish in the steamer or on the rack, cover, and steam for 10–12 minutes, or until the fish is cooked through and flakes easily when tested with a knife.

5 Meanwhile, heat the sunflower oil in a small saucepan over a medium-high heat until shimmering. Scatter the fish with remaining spring onions and ginger, and the garlic, chilli, and lime zest. Drizzle the hot oil over the fish and serve.

serves 2

prep 15 mins
• cook 10–12 mins

steamer, or a wok
with steaming
rack and lid

Pork chops with blue cheese stuffing

This filling is both savoury and sweet and the pecans add
a delightful crunchy texture.

INGREDIENTS
4 lean pork loin chops
1 tbsp olive oil
salt and freshly ground black pepper

For the stuffing
1 dessert apple, such as Cox's, peeled, cored, and finely diced
100g (3^1/$_2$oz) Roquefort cheese or Stilton cheese, crumbled
45g (1^1/$_2$oz) pecans, chopped
2 spring onions, chopped

METHOD
1 Combine the stuffing ingredients and set aside.

2 Trim the skin and excess fat from the pork chops. With a small sharp knife, make a horizontal
slit through the fat side of each chop, cutting through the meat almost to the bone to make
a pocket.

3 Evenly divide the stuffing between the chops, tucking firmly into the pockets. Secure with
wooden cocktail sticks.

4 Preheat the grill on medium-high. Place the pork chops on a baking sheet, brush with oil, and
season with salt and pepper. Grill for 6–8 minutes on each side, depending on thickness, or until
golden brown and the juices run clear. Remove the cocktail sticks and serve.

GOOD WITH Trimmed green beans and new potatoes.

serves 4

prep 10 mins
• cook 12–16 mins

cocktail sticks

Beef with walnut pesto

A great dish for autumn, when fresh walnuts are readily available.

INGREDIENTS
6 beef fillet steaks, about 175g (6oz) each
olive oil, for brushing
salt and freshly ground black pepper

For the walnut pesto
100g (3½oz) walnut pieces
50g (1¾oz) Parmesan cheese, grated
2 garlic cloves
100ml (3½fl oz) olive oil
30g (1oz) tarragon
30g (1oz) flat-leaf parsley
½ tbsp red wine vinegar
salt and freshly ground black pepper

METHOD
1 To make the walnut pesto, fry the walnuts in a dry frying pan for a few minutes, or until toasted, taking care not to burn them. Allow to cool. Place in a food processor with the other pesto ingredients and pulse until coarsely puréed. Season to taste with salt and pepper.

2 Preheat a ridged grill pan or the grill. Brush the steaks with a little olive oil and season well with salt and pepper. Cook them for 2–4 minutes on each side, depending on how you like them. Allow to rest for a few minutes, and serve with a dollop of the walnut pesto on each.

GOOD WITH Roasted sweet potato wedges.

serves 6

prep 15 mins
• cook 8–16 mins

food processor

Pan-fried gammon with pineapple salsa

Gammon is so quick to cook, and this sweet and sour salsa makes the most of its rich flavour.

INGREDIENTS

1 tbsp olive oil
4 gammon steaks
250g can pineapple rings, drained
   and juice reserved
1 tbsp honey
knob of butter
3 tomatoes, skinned and chopped
½ red onion, finely diced

METHOD

1 Heat the oil in a large non-stick frying pan over a high heat. Add the pieces of gammon, and cook for 3–4 minutes on each side, depending on thickness, until golden and cooked through. Remove from the pan, and set aside to keep warm.

2 Immerse the pineapple rings in honey. Melt a knob of butter in the same frying pan. Add the pineapple rings, and cook for a couple of minutes until golden and lightly charred. Remove from the pan, cool slightly, and chop into small pieces.

3 To make the salsa, put the pineapple, tomato, and red onion in a bowl, and mix until combined.

4 To serve, put the reserved pineapple juice into the same pan as used for cooking the pineapple, and let it simmer over a high heat for a few seconds. Pour over the warm gammon steaks, and serve with the salsa.

GOOD WITH Chunky chips or a salad.

serves 4

prep 5 mins
• cook 20 mins

Steak au poivre

This restaurant classic can easily be made at home.

INGREDIENTS

4 sirloin steaks or fillet steaks,
   about 225g (8oz) each
½ tsp mustard powder
1–2 tsp black peppercorns or green
   peppercorns, crushed
2 tbsp sunflower oil
4 tbsp sherry or brandy
150ml (5fl oz) crème fraîche

METHOD

1 Trim any excess fat from the steaks. If using fillet steak, flatten slightly with a meat mallet or rolling pin. Sprinkle with the mustard, then press the peppercorns firmly on both sides of the steaks.

2 Heat a frying pan over a high heat, add the oil, and fry the steaks for 2–3 minutes on each side for a rare steak, 4 minutes for medium, and 5–6 minutes for well done. Remove from the pan to rest.

3 Stir the sherry into the pan juices, add the crème fraîche, and simmer gently, stirring, for 2–3 minutes, or until just reduced. Serve the steaks with the sauce.

GOOD WITH French fries and grilled tomatoes.

serves 4

prep 10 mins
• cook 12 mins

Sweet and sour stir-fried fish with ginger

Crispy coated fish and a flavourful, tangy sauce are perfect partners.

INGREDIENTS

1–2 tbsp cornflour

salt and freshly ground black pepper

675g (1½lb) thick white fish fillets, such as haddock, cut into strips

1–2 tbsp vegetable or sunflower oil

1 onion, roughly chopped

2 garlic cloves, grated or finely chopped

2.5cm (1in) piece of fresh root ginger, finely sliced

large handful mangetout or sugarsnap peas, sliced into strips

For the sweet and sour sauce

1 tbsp white wine vinegar

1 tbsp tomato purée

1 tbsp sugar

1 tsp cornflour

2 tsp light soy sauce

2 tbsp pineapple juice

METHOD

1 First, make the sauce. Mix together the vinegar, tomato purée, sugar, cornflour, soy sauce, and pineapple juice in a jug, and set aside.

2 Put the cornflour on a plate, and season with salt and pepper. Toss the fish in the seasoned flour to coat.

3 In a wok, heat about half of the oil until hot, then add the fish. Stir-fry for about 5 minutes until golden. Remove with a slotted spoon, and set aside to keep warm. Carefully wipe out the wok with kitchen paper, and add a little more oil. When hot, add the onion and stir-fry until it begins to soften, then add the garlic and ginger, and stir-fry for a few minutes more.

4 Pour in the sweet and sour sauce, and let boil for a few minutes, stirring constantly. Reduce the heat to medium, add the mangetout or sugarsnap peas, and stir-fry for 1 minute. Return the fish to the wok, quickly toss together to combine, and serve hot.

GOOD WITH Hot, fluffy rice.

PREPARE AHEAD The sauce can be made 1 day ahead, covered, and kept chilled until ready to use. Cook the fish just before serving, however, or the coating will become soft.

serves 4

prep 10 mins
• cook 20 mins

healthy option

wok

Egg and fennel potato salad

This satisfying salad works best when the potatoes and eggs are still warm.

INGREDIENTS
250g (9oz) new potatoes, scrubbed
4 eggs
drizzle of olive oil
salt and freshly ground black pepper
1 fennel bulb, trimmed and finely chopped
handful of flat-leaf parsley, finely chopped
handful of dill, finely chopped (optional)

METHOD
1 Put the potatoes in a saucepan and cover with boiling water. Lightly salt the water, then cook over a medium heat for 15–20 minutes, or until soft. Drain well.

2 While the potatoes are cooking, place the eggs in a saucepan and cover with water. Bring to the boil, then simmer for 10 minutes, or until hard-boiled (see page 16). Drain, and place the pan under cool running water to stop the eggs from cooking further.

3 Place the potatoes in a serving bowl, drizzle over some olive oil while they are still hot, and season with salt and pepper. Mix in the fennel, parsley, and dill (if using).

4 Drain the eggs, then shell and quarter them. Add to the potato salad, and serve immediately.

serves 4

prep 10 mins
• cook 20 mins

170

Pasta with mushroom sauce

Good-quality mushrooms will make this indulgent dish extra tasty.

INGREDIENTS

4 tbsp olive oil
150g (5½oz) baby button mushrooms
200g (7oz) chestnut mushrooms, finely chopped
125g (4½oz) field mushrooms, grated
1 small glass of dry white wine
3 garlic cloves, grated or finely chopped
salt and freshly ground black pepper
handful of flat-leaf parsley, finely chopped
pinch of mild paprika
300ml (10fl oz) double cream
350g (12oz) dried pappardelle or dried tagliatelle

METHOD

1 Gently heat the oil in a large frying pan, add all the mushrooms, and cook on a low heat for 5 minutes, or until they begin to release their juices. Add the wine, raise the heat, and boil for a couple of minutes. Add the garlic and lots of pepper.

2 Reduce the heat, stir through the parsley and paprika, then pour in the cream and cook, stirring occasionally, on a low heat for 5 minutes.

3 Meanwhile, cook the pasta in a pan of boiling salted water for 10 minutes, or until it is cooked but is still firm to the bite. Drain, keeping back a tiny amount of the cooking water. Return the pasta to the pan and toss together. Taste the sauce and season if needed, then toss with the pasta, and serve.

serves 4

prep 10 mins
• cook 20 mins

Cauliflower cheese

A great comfort food dish that works well as a vegetarian main course.

INGREDIENTS

1 head of cauliflower, outer leaves removed,
   separated into large florets
salt and freshly ground black pepper
100g (3½oz) fresh breadcrumbs

For the cheese sauce

30g (1oz) butter, diced
3 tbsp plain white or wholemeal flour
1½ tsp mustard powder
450ml (15fl oz) milk
125g (4½oz) mature Cheddar cheese, grated
salt and freshly ground black pepper

METHOD

1 Bring a large saucepan of salted water to the boil. Add the cauliflower florets and boil for 7 minutes, or until just tender. Drain well and rinse with cold water to stop the cooking. Arrange the florets in an ovenproof serving dish.

2 Preheat the grill on its highest setting. To make the cheese sauce, melt the butter in a pan over a low heat, add the flour and mustard powder, and stir to combine. Cook for 2 minutes, stirring all the time. Remove from the heat, add the milk, and stir constantly until smooth. Return to the heat and bring slowly to the boil, then reduce the heat and simmer to thicken for 1–2 minutes. Remove the pan from the heat and stir in three-quarters of the cheese until melted. Season to taste with salt and pepper, then pour the sauce over the florets.

3 Toss the remaining cheese with the breadcrumbs and sprinkle over the florets. Place the dish under the grill for 10 minutes, or until the sauce bubbles and the top is golden. Serve hot from the dish.

GOOD WITH Any roast meat, grilled bacon, or sausages.

serves 4–6

prep 10 mins
• cook 20 mins

Caramelized pork tenderloin with pecan nuts and apricots

Pork works brilliantly with sweet, fruity flavours – the dash of whisky is a delightful twist.

INGREDIENTS

1–2 tsp brown sugar
675g (1½lb) pork tenderloin
  (in one piece)
1 tbsp olive oil
knob of butter
handful of pecan nuts
handful of dried apricots, halved
splash of whisky (optional)
300ml (10fl oz) double cream

METHOD

1 Rub the brown sugar over the pork, then slice it horizontally into medallions.

2 Heat the oil and butter in a frying pan over a medium-high heat. Brown the pork medallions for 3–4 minutes on each side until golden. Add the pecans and apricots, and cook for a few more minutes.

3 Increase the heat to high, and add the whisky (if using). Let it simmer for a couple of minutes until the alcohol has evaporated. Reduce the heat to medium, pour over the cream, and let it simmer for a few minutes more. Serve hot.

GOOD WITH Creamy mashed potatoes.

serves 4

prep 10 mins
• cook 15 mins

Hamburgers

Burgers are classic American fare and always leave you satisfied.

INGREDIENTS

450g (1lb) lean minced steak
½ onion, very finely chopped
1 egg yolk
salt and freshly ground black pepper
olive oil or sunflower oil
4 sesame seed buns, cut in half and lightly toasted

METHOD

1 Place the minced beef and chopped onions in a mixing bowl, add the egg yolk, season to taste with salt and pepper, and mix well.

2 Divide the mixture into 4 equal portions and, using wet hands, shape them into 4 burgers.

3 Preheat a ridged grill pan or grill on its highest setting. Lightly oil the ridged grill pan and grill the burgers for 3 minutes on each side, or longer if you prefer.

4 Serve in toasted sesame seed buns with your favourite toppings.

GOOD WITH Sliced onions, sliced tomatoes, lettuce, pickles, tomato ketchup, mayonnaise, and mustard.

PREPARE AHEAD You can make the burgers 1 day in advance. Wrap them tightly in cling film and chill until ready to cook.

serves 4

prep 15 mins
• cook 10 mins

freeze the
uncooked
hamburgers for
up to 3 months

Seared duck with five-spice and noodles

Tender, pan-fried duck with fragrant five-spice, orange, and coriander.

INGREDIENTS
4 duck breasts, about 150g (5½oz) each,
   skin on and scored in a crisscross pattern
2–3 tsp five-spice paste
knob of butter
2 tbsp freshly squeezed orange juice
1 tsp soft brown sugar
250g packet ready-to-wok noodles
handful of coriander, finely chopped

METHOD
1 Rub the duck breasts in the five-spice paste. Melt the butter in a frying pan over a high heat. Add the duck breasts, skin-side down, and cook for about 10 minutes until the skin is golden and crisp. Carefully pour the fat away from the pan, then turn the breasts over and cook on the other side for a further 8 minutes.

2 Remove the meat from the pan, cut into slices, and arrange on a warm plate. Pour away any remaining fat, then add the orange juice to the pan along with the sugar. Let it simmer for a minute or two, scraping up any bits from the bottom of the pan with a wooden spoon.

3 Add the noodles, and toss them in the sauce for a couple of minutes. Remove from the heat, and stir through the coriander. Serve immediately with the warm duck breasts.

serves 4

prep 10 mins
• cook 20 mins

Turkey burgers

This is a sensible choice if you want a healthier alternative to a beef burger.

INGREDIENTS

675g (1½lb) turkey mince
handful of thyme, leaves only, finely chopped
grated zest and juice of 1 lemon
1 red chilli, deseeded and finely chopped
salt and freshly ground black pepper
knob of butter, melted
2 tbsp plain flour, to dust
olive oil or vegetable oil for frying
4 hamburger or other bread buns, to serve

METHOD

1 Put the turkey mince, thyme, lemon zest and juice, and chilli in a bowl. Season well with salt and pepper. Mix together until well combined.

2 Now add the melted butter and, using your hands, work the mixture until it all sticks together. Divide the mixture into four, then scoop up each portion, and form into a ball. Press flat with your hands to form a burger. Dust with the flour, then chill in the refrigerator for 5–10 minutes to firm up.

3 Heat a little olive or vegetable oil in a non-stick frying pan over a medium-high heat. Fry the burgers for about 4 minutes on each side until golden and cooked through. Serve in a bun with crisp lettuce, slices of tomato, and a dollop of mayonnaise.

GOOD WITH Crisp iceburg lettuce, tomato slices, and mayonnaise.

PREPARE AHEAD You can make the burgers 1 day in advance. Wrap them tightly in cling film and chill until needed.

serves 4

prep 15 mins
• cook 15 mins

Pork escalopes with breadcrumb and parsley crust

Flattening meat helps it to cook quickly and evenly; this is also a good technique to try with chicken, turkey, and veal.

INGREDIENTS

75g (2¹/₂oz) breadcrumbs, toasted
handful of flat-leaf parsley, finely chopped
salt and freshly ground black pepper
2 large pork steak fillets, 175–225g (6–8oz) each
1–2 eggs, beaten
1–2 tbsp plain flour
1–2 tbsp olive oil
1 small glass of dry white wine

METHOD

1 In a bowl, mix the breadcrumbs and parsley, and season well with salt and pepper. Halve each piece of pork, then sandwich each one between two sheets of cling film. Bash with a meat mallet or the side of a rolling pin until thin and of an even thickness. Season well with salt and pepper.

2 Put the egg, flour, and breadcrumbs each on separate plates. Coat each piece of pork first in the flour, then the egg, and lastly the breadcrumbs. Heat half of the oil in a large non-stick frying pan over a high heat. Add 2 of the pork escalopes, and cook for 3–4 minutes on each side until golden and cooked through. Remove from the pan, sit on kitchen paper, and set aside to keep warm while you cook the remaining 2 escalopes. Keep warm while making the sauce.

3 To make the sauce, tip the wine into the same frying pan, and scrape up all the crispy bits from the bottom with a wooden spoon. Let simmer until the alcohol has evaporated, then pour over the pork. Serve immediately.

GOOD WITH A spinach and tomato salad, or rocket drizzled with a little lemon juice.

serves 4

prep 15 mins
• cook 15 mins

Thai-style minced pork

Low in fat, this tasty and speedy stir-fry is a perfect family supper dish.

INGREDIENTS
1 tbsp vegetable oil
675g (1½lb) pork mince
4 garlic cloves, grated or finely chopped
pinch of salt
2 red chillies, deseeded and finely chopped
juice of 1 lime
1 tbsp Thai fish sauce, such as nam pla
1 tbsp dark soy sauce
handful of coriander, finely chopped
medium rice noodles or rice, to serve

METHOD
1 Heat the oil in a wok or large frying pan over a medium-high heat. Add the pork, garlic, and a pinch of salt. Stir-fry until no longer pink, tossing continuously.

2 Add the chillies, lime juice, fish sauce, and soy sauce, and stir-fry for a further 5 minutes.

3 When ready to serve, sprinkle over the coriander, and stir well. Serve hot with noodles or rice.

serves 4

prep 10 mins
• cook 15 mins

healthy option

Hot and sour beef stir-fry with green beans

A tangy and spicy Chinese-style dish.

INGREDIENTS

1 tbsp clear honey
splash of Thai fish sauce, such as nam pla
675g (1½lb) rump steak, cut into
   thin strips
handful of fine green beans, trimmed
1 tbsp sesame oil
rice or noodles, to serve

For the hot and sour sauce

2 garlic cloves, grated or
   finely chopped
1 tsp dark soft brown sugar
6 salted brown anchovy
   fillets, chopped
3 red chillies, deseeded and finely chopped
splash of Chinese rice wine
juice of 1 lime
salt

METHOD

1 First, make the hot and sour sauce. Using a mortar and pestle, pound all the ingredients, except the rice wine and lime juice, into a smooth paste. Add the lime juice slowly, tasting as you go, and season with salt. Set aside.

2 Put the honey and fish sauce in a bowl, add the steak, and combine well. Blanch the beans in a pan of boiling salted water for a few minutes, then drain and refresh in cold water.

3 Heat the oil in a wok or large frying pan over a medium-high heat. Add the steak, and stir-fry, tossing the meat constantly, for 3–5 minutes until it is sealed and cooked. Remove with a slotted spoon, and set aside.

4 Add the hot and sour sauce to the wok or frying pan, and stir for a couple of minutes. Return the meat to the pan, and throw in the beans. Increase the heat to high, add the rice wine, and let boil for a minute or two. Serve immediately with the rice or noodles.

serves 4

prep 10 mins
• cook 20 mins

healthy option

mortar and pestle

189

QUICK PUDDINGS

Zabaglione

This Italian pudding was invented by a happy accident in the 17th century when wine was poured into egg custard.

INGREDIENTS

4 egg yolks
4 tbsp caster sugar
8 tbsp Marsala
finely grated zest of 1 orange
8 sponge fingers or biscotti, to serve

METHOD

1 Bring a large saucepan of water to the boil, then lower the heat to simmer.

2 Put the egg yolks, sugar, Marsala, and half the orange zest into a large glass or china bowl and place on top of the pan of simmering water. Start to whisk immediately, using a balloon whisk. Keep whisking for 5–10 minutes, or until the mixture is pale, thick, fluffy, and warmed through.

3 Pour into 4 cocktail glasses and decorate with the remaining orange zest; serve immediately with sponge fingers or biscotti.

serves 4

prep 5 mins
• cook 10 mins

Eton mess

Culinary legend maintains that this medley was created after a schoolboy dropped a picnic hamper.

INGREDIENTS

350g (12oz) ripe strawberries, sliced
2 tbsp caster sugar
2 tbsp orange juice or orange-flavoured liqueur
300ml (10fl oz) double cream
125g (4½oz) ready-baked meringue nests

METHOD

1 Put the strawberries in a bowl, sprinkle the sugar over, add the orange juice, then use a fork to crush the mixture.

2 Whip the cream until stiff peaks begin to form. Crush the meringue nests into small pieces.

3 Stir the meringue into the whipped cream. Top with the berries and the juices, and stir together. Serve immediately.

GOOD WITH Fresh raspberries and/or blueberries scattered over the top.

PREPARE AHEAD Steps 1 and 2 can be completed several hours in advance. Assemble the pudding just before serving.

serves 4

prep 10 mins

Baked figs with cinnamon and honey

A simple-to-prepare, but stylish, end to a meal.

INGREDIENTS
6 firm figs
2 tbsp clear honey
2 tbsp brandy or rum
ground cinnamon, for sprinkling

METHOD
1 Preheat the oven to 180°C (350°F/Gas 4). Cut the figs in half and place closely together in a shallow baking dish or roasting tin.

2 Drizzle over the honey and brandy, and sprinkle each fig with a generous pinch of cinnamon.

3 Bake for 20 minutes, or until softened. Check the figs after 10 minutes, as they may differ in ripeness slightly and require different cooking times. Serve warm or at room temperature.

GOOD WITH Mascarpone, vanilla ice cream, or crème fraîche.

serves 4

prep 2–3 mins
• cook 20 mins

Warm fruit compôte

An ideal dish when supplies of fresh fruit are limited.

INGREDIENTS
30g (1oz) butter
6 prunes, chopped
6 dried apricots, chopped
2 large apples, peeled, cored, and chopped
1 firm pear, peeled, cored, and chopped
1 cinnamon stick
2 tsp sugar
2 tsp lemon juice
yogurt and honey, to serve

METHOD
1 Melt the butter in a heavy saucepan over a medium heat. Add the fruit and cinnamon stick. Cook gently, stirring often, until the fruit has completely softened.

2 Stir in the sugar and heat for a further couple of minutes, or until the sugar has dissolved.

3 Remove the pan from the heat, sprinkle with lemon juice, and serve warm with a spoonful of yogurt and a drizzle of honey.

PREPARE AHEAD The compôte can be made up to 3 days in advance, covered, and refrigerated.

serves 4

prep 10 mins
• cook 5–10 mins

Berries with citrus syrup

Juicy seasonal berries are made even more luscious with a sweet lemon-orange syrup.

INGREDIENTS

500g (1lb 2oz) mixed red berries, such as
   raspberries, strawberries, and redcurrants
125g (4½oz) caster sugar
zest of 1 lemon, cut into strips
1 tbsp orange juice
handful of mint leaves

METHOD

1 Place the mixed berries in a serving dish and set aside.

2 Mix the sugar with 120ml (4fl oz) water in a heavy-based saucepan. Heat slowly until the sugar has dissolved, stirring occasionally, then increase the heat, and boil for 5 minutes. Remove the pan from the heat and leave to cool, then add the lemon zest and orange juice.

3 Drizzle the syrup over the berries, then add the mint leaves. Leave to macerate for 10 minutes, before serving.

GOOD WITH Whipped cream or ice cream.

PREPARE AHEAD The dish can be made up to 1 hour in advance.

serves 4

prep 5 mins,
plus macerating
• cook 10 mins

healthy option

Honey-baked apricots with mascarpone

This Italian dessert, made here with canned fruit, can be enjoyed all year round.

INGREDIENTS

400g can apricots, drained
3 tbsp clear honey
3 tbsp flaked almonds
pinch of ground ginger or cinnamon
150g (5^1/$_2$oz) mascarpone, chilled to serve

METHOD

1 Preheat the grill on its highest setting, and lightly butter the bottom and sides of an ovenproof dish large enough to hold all the apricot halves in a single layer.

2 Put the apricots in the dish, cut-sides up. Brush with the honey, then scatter over the almonds, and very lightly dust with the ground ginger.

3 Grill for 10 minutes, or until the apricots are tender when pierced with the tip of a knife and the almonds are toasted. Serve the apricots hot or cool with the chilled mascarpone on the side.

GOOD WITH Vanilla ice cream or thick whipped cream instead of the mascarpone.

PREPARE AHEAD The dish can be assembled, ready for baking, several hours in advance.

serves 4

prep 10 mins
• cook 10 mins

Mango and papaya salad

The fruit salad is taken to new heights with exotic fruit and a ginger dressing.

INGREDIENTS

1 piece of preserved stem ginger, cut into thin strips
2 tbsp stem ginger syrup
2 tbsp caster sugar
grated zest and juice of 1 lemon
1 pomegranate, cut in half, seeds scooped out
1 large ripe mango
1 large ripe papaya fruit
1 small ogen melon
lime wedges, to serve

METHOD

1 Place the ginger, ginger syrup, sugar, and 120ml (4fl oz) of water into a saucepan, and heat gently, stirring occasionally. Bring to the boil, then simmer gently for 5–6 minutes. Remove from the heat, and stir in the lemon zest and juice and the pomegranate seeds.

2 Peel the mango and use a sharp knife to cut the flesh away from the stone. Cut it into slices. Halve, deseed, and peel the papaya, then cut into wedges. Halve and deseed the melon, cut into wedges, and peel, then cut the flesh into bite-sized chunks. Arrange the mango, papaya, and melon on a large serving platter.

3 Pour the pomegranate and ginger dressing over the fruit, and serve with lime wedges to squeeze over.

GOOD WITH Greek yogurt or whipped cream.

PREPARE AHEAD The dressing can be made and kept in a refrigerator for up to 2 days in advance. The fruit can be prepared up to 24 hours in advance and chilled until required.

serves 4

prep 15 mins
• cook 10 mins

healthy option

Pineapple flambé

Rings of fresh pineapple flambéd in rum or brandy make a smart restaurant-style dessert.

INGREDIENTS

1 pineapple
4 tbsp dark rum or brandy
2 tbsp fresh lime juice
50g (1¾oz) salted butter
50g (1¾oz) light soft brown sugar
whipped cream, to serve
ground cinnamon, for dusting

METHOD

1 Peel and thinly slice the pineapple. Cut out the tough core using a small round cutter or the lip of a sharp knife.

2 Put the pineapple slices and any pineapple juice into a large frying pan with the rum and lime juice, and heat. Light the alcohol by carefully tilting the pan into the gas flame, or by using a match, and allow the flames to die down.

3 Dot the pineapple with butter and sprinkle with sugar. Shake the pan while heating gently, until the butter melts, the sugar dissolves, and the mixture thickens to a glaze. Serve with whipped cream and a dusting of ground cinnamon.

GOOD WITH Mascarpone or ice cream.

serves 4

prep 15–20 mins
• cook 10 mins

Citrus fruit salad

Refreshing, colourful, and full of vitamins, this pretty dessert is sunshine in a bowl.

INGREDIENTS

3 oranges
1 grapefruit
1 ruby grapefruit
2 clementines or mandarins
juice of 1 lime
1–2 tbsp sugar (optional)
lime zest, to decorate (optional)

METHOD

1 Using a small, sharp knife, cut away the skin and all the pith from the oranges and grapefruit. Cutting towards the centre of the fruit, remove each segment from its membrane (see page 18).

2 Place all the segments in a bowl, squeeze any juice from the membranes into the bowl, and discard the membranes.

3 Peel the clementines and divide into segments. Add to the bowl, then add the lime juice, and stir to coat. Sprinkle with sugar to taste (if using), then chill in the refrigerator until ready to serve.

4 Before serving, strain off any excess juice (this can be served separately as a refreshing drink) and sprinkle with lime zest, if using.

PREPARE AHEAD You can assemble the fruit salad up to 24 hours in advance. Cover and refrigerate until needed.

serves 4

prep 20 mins

healthy option

Pear gratin

A sophisticated, simple, and foolproof dessert.

INGREDIENTS

4 ripe Comice pears
150g (5½oz) blackberries
60g (2oz) walnuts, roughly chopped
225g (8oz) mascarpone
30g (1oz) dark muscovado sugar

METHOD

1 Preheat the grill on its highest setting. Quarter the pears and remove the cores. Place them skin-side down into a shallow flameproof dish. Scatter over the blackberries and walnuts.

2 Drop spoonfuls of mascarpone over the pears and sprinkle the sugar on top. Grill for 3–5 minutes, or until the mascarpone is hot and bubbling, and the sugar begins to caramelize.

GOOD WITH Crisp buttery biscuits.

serves 4

prep 10 mins
• cook 3–5 mins

Strawberry mousse

This speedy dessert is bound to be a favourite with the kids.

INGREDIENTS

450g (1lb) ripe strawberries
175g can evaporated milk, well chilled
30g (1oz) caster sugar
200g (7oz) Greek yogurt, plus extra to serve

METHOD

1 Slice a strawberry and set aside for decoration. Divide half the strawberries between 4 glasses and place the remaining strawberries into a food processor and blend to a purée. Push through a sieve to remove the seeds. If you do not have a food processor, mash with a fork before pushing through a sieve.

2 Using an electric whisk, whisk the milk in a large bowl until doubled in volume, which will take 6–8 minutes. Whisk in the sugar and stir in the strawberry purée and Greek yogurt until well combined. Spoon the whisked mixture into the glasses and chill for 15–20 minutes.

3 Serve decorated with a little extra yogurt and the reserved strawberry slices.

PREPARE AHEAD The mousse can be made several hours in advance.

serves 4

prep 15 mins,
plus chilling

electric whisk

the mousse
can be frozen
in individual
freezerproof
dishes for up
to 3 months

Pear and grape salad

Cucumber is not often added to sweet dishes, but it works perfectly in this exotic fruit salad.

INGREDIENTS

1 cucumber
2 stalks lemongrass
85g (3oz) golden caster sugar
2 ripe red-skinned pears
125g (4½oz) green seedless grapes
125g (4½oz) red seedless grapes
small handful of mint leaves

METHOD

1 Trim the ends from the cucumber. Cut it in half lengthways, scoop out and discard the seeds using a teaspoon, then slice thinly. Remove any tough outer leaves from the lemongrass stalks and discard. Halve lengthways and bash with a rolling pin.

2 Place the lemongrass in a saucepan with the sugar and 200ml (7fl oz) water, and heat gently until the sugar has dissolved. Bring to the boil and boil for 1 minute, then remove from the heat and stir in the cucumber. Allow to cool.

3 Discard the lemongrass. Quarter the pears and discard the cores, then cut the flesh into thin wedges, and add to the syrup with the grapes. To serve, transfer to a serving dish and scatter over the mint leaves.

GOOD WITH Plain yogurt or Greek yogurt.

PREPARE AHEAD The salad can be made in advance, and stored in the refrigerator.

serves 4

prep 10 mins
• cook 5–6 mins

Chocolate-dipped fruits

This decadent treat is perfect with after-dinner drinks.

INGREDIENTS

12 physalis (Cape gooseberries)
12 strawberries
100g (3½oz) good-quality dark chocolate

METHOD

1 Pull back the papery leaves of each physalis to expose the round orange fruit. Leave the stalks on the strawberries. Line a flat tray or plate with greaseproof paper.

2 Break up the chocolate and place it in a heatproof bowl over a pan of barely simmering water and stir occasionally for 8–10 minutes, or until melted and smooth.

3 Holding the fruit by the stalks, dip each fruit into the chocolate and place on the greaseproof paper. Work quickly, as the chocolate does not take long to set.

4 Chill in the refrigerator until the chocolate is set.

PREPARE AHEAD These can be prepared up to 24 hours in advance and kept refrigerated.

serves 4

prep 20 mins,
plus chilling
• cook 10 mins

Knickerbocker glory

A childhood favourite, with ice cream, fruit, cream, and sauce. It is traditionally served layered in tall glasses.

INGREDIENTS

2 peaches
8 small scoops strawberry ice cream
8 tbsp strawberry ice cream sauce
4 small scoops chocolate ice cream
150ml (5fl oz) double cream, whipped
1 tbsp sugar strands or sugar balls
4 maraschino cherries
wafer biscuits, to serve

METHOD

1 Place the peaches in a pan of boiling water for 30 seconds to loosen the skins. Drain and halve the fruit, discarding the stones, then peel. Cut the flesh into wedges and place a few into the base of 4 tall glasses or sundae dishes. Top with a scoop of strawberry ice cream and a drizzle of strawberry sauce.

2 Repeat the layering with the remaining peach slices, strawberry ice cream, and strawberry sauce. Place a scoop of chocolate ice cream on top.

3 Place a spoonful of whipped cream to one side of the chocolate ice cream and sprinkle with sugar strands. Decorate with a maraschino cherry and serve each with wafer biscuits.

serves 4

prep 15 mins

Banoffee pie

Always a hit, this dessert's name derives from its delicious filling of fresh bananas and toffee sauce.

INGREDIENTS

20cm ready-made tart case
200g (7oz) ready-made thick caramel sauce
   (such as Dulce de leche)
2–3 ripe bananas
300ml (10fl oz) double cream
   or whipping cream
25g (scant 1oz) dark chocolate

METHOD

1 Place the tart case on a serving plate. Spoon in the caramel sauce and spread evenly. Slice the bananas and scatter over the top.

2 Put the cream in a bowl and whisk with an electric hand whisk until soft peaks form, then spoon over the bananas. Grate the chocolate over the top and serve.

serves 8

prep 15 mins

**hand-held
electric whisk**

ACKNOWLEDGMENTS

DORLING KINDERSLEY WOULD LIKE TO THANK THE FOLLOWING:

Photographers
Carole Tuff, Tony Cambio, William Shaw, Stuart West, David Munns, David Murray,
Adrian Heapy, Nigel Gibson, Kieran Watson, Roddy Paine, Gavin Sawyer, Ian O'Leary,
Steve Baxter, Martin Brigdale, Francesco Guillamet, Jeff Kauck, William Reavell, Jon Whitaker

Picture Researcher
Emma Shepherd

Proofreader
Anna Osborn

Indexer
Susan Bosanko

Useful information

Refrigerator and freezer storage guidelines

FOOD	REFRIGERATOR	FREEZER
Raw poultry, fish, and meat (small pieces)	2–3 days	3 months
Raw minced beef and poultry	1–3 days	3 months
Cooked whole roasts or whole poultry	2–3 days	9 months
Cooked poultry pieces	2–3 days	3 months
Soups and stocks	2–3 days	3–6 months
Stews	2–3 days	3 months
Pies	2–3 days	3–6 months

Oven temperature equivalents

CELSIUS	FAHRENHEIT	GAS	DESCRIPTION
110°C	225°F	$1/4$	Cool
130°C	250°F	$1/2$	Cool
140°C	275°F	1	Very low
150°C	300°F	2	Very low
160°C	325°F	3	Low
180°C	350°F	4	Moderate
190°C	375°F	5	Moderately hot
200°C	400°F	6	Hot
220°C	425°F	7	Hot
230°C	450°F	8	Very hot
240°C	475°F	9	Very hot